Library of
Davidson College

KNOWING GOD: RELIGIOUS KNOWLEDGE IN THE THEOLOGY OF JOHN BAILLIE

William Powell Tuck

University Press of America™

Copyright © 1978 by

University Press of America™

division of
R.F. Publishing, Inc.
4710 Auth Place, S.E., Washington, D.C. 20023

All rights reserved
Printed in the United States of America

231
B15xt

ISBN: 0-8191-0484-1

82-4189

ACKNOWLEDGMENT

Grateful acknowledgment is made to the following publishers for permission to quote material from their sources:

Excerpts from the works of John Baillie are used with the permission of Charles Scribner's Sons and are fully protected by copyright.
From GOD'S WILL IN OUR TIME edited by John Baillie. Copyright 1942. Used by permission of SCM Press, Ltd.
From THE IDEA OF REVELATION IN RECENT THOUGHT by John Baillie. Copyright 1956. Used by permission of Columbia University Press.
From INTERNATIONAL REVIEW OF MISSION, "World Mission of the Church: The Contemporary Scene," by John Baillie (Vol. 41, April, 1952) and "The Given Word: The Message of the Unvarying Gospel," by John Baillie (Vol. 36, October, 1947). Used by permission.
From THE INTERPRETATION OF RELIGION by John Baillie. Copyright 1929. Used by permission of T. & T. Clark, Ltd.
From UNION SEMINARY QUARTERLY REVIEW, "Why I Believe in God" by John Baillie (Vol. 3, March, 1948) and "A Conversation Resumed: Some Reflections on Recent Lenguistic Philosophy," by Brian Gerrish (Vol. 13, March, 1958). Used by permission.

From FOUNDATIONS OF CHRISTIAN KNOWLEDGE by George Harkness. Copyright © 1955 by Pierce and Washabaugh, and THE RELIGIOUS TEACHINGS OF THE OLD TESTAMENT by Albert C. Knudson. Copyright 1918. Used by permission of Abingdon Press.
From CHRISTIAN DOCTRINE by J. S. Whale. Copyright 1941. Used by permission of the Cambridge University Press.
From FOUNDATIONS, "Baptists and Sources of Authority," by Bernard Ramm (I:July, 1958). Used by permission.
From OUR EXPERIENCE OF GOD by H. D. Lewis. Copyright 1959. Used by permission of George Allen & Unwin Ltd.
From THE NEW QUEST by Rufus Jones. Used by permission from the Girard Trust Company, Philadelphia, Pennsylvania.
From PHILOSOPHY OF RELIGION by Elton Trueblood. Copyright 1957; THE CHRISTIAN UNDERSTANDING OF GOD by Nels F. S. Ferré. Copyright 1951; and OLD TESTAMENT THEOLOGY, Vol. I, by Gerhard Von Rad. Copyright 1962. Used by permission of Harper & Row Publishers.
From BAPTISTS CONFESSIONS OF FAITH by William L. Lumpkin. Copyright 1959. Used by permission of Judson Press.
From THE LIFE AND FAITH OF THE BAPTISTS by H. Wheeler Robinson. Copyright 1946. Used by permission of The Kingsgate Press.
From ADVENTURES OF IDEAS by Alfred North Whitehead. Copyright

1933, renewed 1961 by Evelyn Whitehead. Used by permission of Macmillan Publishing Co., Inc.

From NATURE, MAN AND GOD by William Temple, and BAPTISM IN THE NEW TESTAMENT by George R. Beasley-Murray. Used by permission of Macmillan, London and Basingstoke.

From CHURCH DOGMATICS, I, I and Vol. IV, part 4- Fragment by Karl Barth. Copyright 1956 and 1969. Used by permission of T. & T. Clark, Ltd.

From SYSTEMATIC THEOLOGY, Vol. I, by Paul Tillich. Copyright 1951, and THE PROTESTANT ERA by Paul Tillich. Copyright 1957. Used by permission of the University of Chicago Press.

From THE INSPIRATION OF SCRIPTURE by Dewey M. Beegle. Copyright © MCMLXIII, W. L. Jenkins. Used by permission of the Westminster Press.

All Scripture quotations are from the Revised Standard Version of the Bible. Copyrighted 1946, 1952, © 1971 and 1973. Used by permission of the International Council of Religious Education of the National Council of the Churches of Christ.

To

Emily

who has enhanced

my religious knowledge

TABLE OF CONTENTS

CHAPTER		PAGE
PREFACE		
I.	THE PROBLEM OF RELIGIOUS KNOWLEDGE	1
	The Possibility of Knowledge	1
	Kinds of Knowledge	5
	Is Religious Knowledge Possible?	8
II.	GENERAL KNOWLEDGE OF GOD	13
	The Nature of Religious Knowledge	13
	Epistemological Status of Natural Religion	23
	Human Discovery and Divine Revelation	26
III.	SPECIAL KNOWLEDGE OF GOD	29
	The Nature and Content of Revelation	29
	The Reception of Revelation	38
	Faith as Apprehension and Response	42
IV.	RELIGIOUS KNOWLEDGE AND THE LANGUAGE OF FAITH	61
	The Role of the Bible in Religious Knowledge	61
	The Role of Language in Religious Knowledge	65
	The Verification of Religious Knowledge	71
V.	THE PRACTICAL AFFIRMATION OF RELIGIOUS KNOWLEDGE	79
	The Christian Frame of Reference	79
	Religious Knowledge and Morality	85
	The Challenge of Revelation	90
VI.	SUMMARY AND CONCLUSIONS	93
	A Summary of Baillie's Concept of Religious Knowledge	93
	The Positive Values in Baillie's Concepts of Religious Knowledge	97
	Objections to Baillie's Concept of Religious Knowledge	100
	Conclusion	102
NOTES		103

CHAPTER	PAGE
BIBLIOGRAPHY	123
A. Writings of Baillie	123
B. Other Selected Sources	126
Index of Names	133
Index of Subjects	135
About The Author	139

PREFACE

Theology has undergone a whirlwind of trends and challenges in the past decade. Some of the voices, in a frank appraisal of contemporary culture, assert that not only are theological statements meaningless but that the demise of God himself has begun. Joining the "new radical" voices in a rapidly changing society were many new sounds blowing in the winds of change - the Secularist, the New Morality, the New Hermeneutic, an orientation toward the future with apocalyptic and eschatological expectations, along with theologies of black liberation, revolution, ecology, play and celebration, as well as an explosion of liturgical renewal. At the heart of all this struggle is the radical matter of whether one can "know" God and interpret this experience meaningfully to another. "The problem of revelation," declares Wolfhart Pannenberg, "has become the fundamental question in modern theology."[1] The volume of material written from many theological perspectives on the problem of religious knowledge attests to the significance of this problem in contemporary religious thought.

Early in his life the problem of religious knowledge became the predominant concern of John Baillie, and most of his major writings have been directed toward this specific problem. Although Baillie was a prolific writer, his work is not characterized by a systematic quality like the writings of Karl Barth or Paul Tillich. Instead of a systematic comprehensiveness, his thought has been focused on specific, theological problems. The question of religious knowledge was his chief concern and to it he gave his life's work. Since the problem of religious knowledge is still one of the central questions in contemporary theology, it could prove helpful to study a theologian whose major emphasis was devoted to casting some light on this very subject. It has been eighteen years since John Baillie died on September 29, 1960, and the time is ripe for an evaluation of his theological contribution.

As a theologian Baillie held a mediating position between liberal and dialectical theology. In a sense his theological approach has been overlooked by many recently because Baillie has been so quickly deposited in the Barthian camp. However, in an autobiographical sketch, he indicates that he learned much from the "Theology of Crisis," but that he still remains a "Christian Platonist."[2] He observes that he and Barth studied at Marburg at very nearly the same time but "we must have been attracted and repelled by very different sides of our teacher's thought."[3] Throughout much of his writing, Baillie is often in debate with Barth, the "grandfather" of much modern theology.

i

The numerous books and articles written by Baillie combined a fine sense of scholarship with a deep devotional spirit. He held many places of esteem in educational and ecclesiastical circles including theological chairs at Auburn Theological Seminary in New York; Emmanuel College, Toronto, Canada; Union Theological Seminary in New York, and Professor of Divinity in Edinburgh University. He also served as Principal of New College and Dean of the Faculty of Divinity at Edinburgh University, one of the Presidents of the World Council of Churches, and Chaplain to the Queen in Scotland.

Many of contemporary theologians, such as Gerhart Ebeling, Jürgen Moltmann, Wolfhart Pannenberg, and others, reflect insights which have emerged out of a response, at least partially, to whether or not man is able to discern any knowledge of God in the modern world. Although they have moved beyond Baillie in some areas, have challenged theses similar to his, and have probed questions which have arisen out of technology, the rapidity of change, the revolutionary and ecological crises, etc., his predominant life-long concern with the issue of religious knowledge is still the most significant question in Christian theology today. In this study I have selected not to compare Baillie's concept of religious knowledge with the theologians of a decade after his death, but have chosen, instead, to reflect his quest for understanding religious knowledge off of his own contemporaries. These were the giants of his own day and he struggled with them in a real intellectual combat for truth.

I want to express my appreciation to Mrs. F. S. Paris for her typing of the original manuscript and her meticulous care in preparing the final copy. I am indebted to my wife, Emily, for her support and encouragement in this work in its formative stages and for her invaluable advice and counsel throughout the writing of it. I would be derelict if I did not express my appreciation to Dr. Stewart A. Newman, Professor Emeritus of Theology and Philosophy of Religion at Southeastern Baptist Theological Seminary, Wake Forest, North Carolina, who first introduced me to Baillie's thought, and to Dr. William A. Mueller, Professor Emeritus of the New Orleans Baptist Theological Seminary and Dr. Robert R. Soileau, presently Professor of Sociology at Louisiana State University, Baton Rouge, Louisiana, who enheartened me in my study of Baillie when the end seemed evasive. I also want to thank Dr. Frank Stagg, James Buchanan Harrison Professor of New Testament Interpretation, Southern Baptist Theological Seminary, Louisville, Kentucky, and a former student of John Baillie at Edinburgh, for reading the manuscript and encouraging me to publish it.

CHAPTER I

THE PROBLEM OF RELIGIOUS KNOWLEDGE

Many of the greatest theological and philosophical minds of the centuries have applied their energies in an effort to reach an adequate solution to the problem of religious knowledge. Our first concern will be directed toward the epistemological approach that Baillie takes toward this problem. An inquiry into the possibility of knowledge in general is necessary before attention can be directed to the possibility of religious knowledge in particular.

I. THE POSSIBILITY OF KNOWLEDGE

Socrates, Plato, Aristotle, and other ancient Greek philosophers have asserted that all men by nature desire to know. From ancient philosophy to medieval philosophy and into the modern philosophical thought of Descartes, Locke, Hume, Kant, and Hegel, the question of knowledge has undergone penetrating inquiry. Many of the world's best minds have contended that man has the possibility of knowledge. Few have been willing to accept the position of the Sophist that knowledge is unattainable. From Descartes' famous claim, "<u>cogito, ergo sum,</u>" to Locke, Berkeley, and Hume's empirical theory of knowledge, philosophers have attempted to set forth a theory of knowledge that is both consistent and credible. No theory has been without its inconsistencies, but still the claim to know has been maintained.

What is it that man claims to know? David Elton Trueblood enumerates six supposed objects of human knowledge that are most prominent in philosophical inquiry.

The first supposed object of human knowledge is that of bodies. A body is anything which has location and mass.

The second object of knowledge is that of other minds. Man is able to have genuine communication with objects which are independent of himself such as trees and stones, yet the character of which is different from stones and trees.

The third object of knowledge is one's own mind. Here man has direct awareness. He alone is the self-conscious animal. Here under this category of alleged objects of knowledge, Trueblood has set forth a convincing statement about the possibility of knowledge apart from sensory origin.

Thus, we find a series of steps in the direction of independence. In knowledge of bodies the object is physical, in knowledge of other minds the knowledge is mediated by physical acts, but in knowledge of self, where the same being is both knower and known, the knowledge is immediate. Knowledge of one's own thoughts proves the possibility of knowledge apart from the senses. By what sensory experience am I aware of my experience of repentance which I felt so keenly ten minutes ago? Certainly not by hearing, by seeing, by touch, or by any other sense impression at all. That knowledge of one's own thoughts, including those of the immediate past, is real knowledge there is no doubt. This is bound to pose a serious problem for those who claim dogmatically that the only possible knowledge is sensory in origin.[1]

A fourth class of objects of human knowledge is that of historical events. Through secondary evidence inferences are made concerning events that occurred in the past.

The fifth class of objects of human knowledge is concerned with universals. Knowledge cannot be confined to mere particulars. All knowledge of truth involves some knowledge of universals.

The final class of objects of human knowledge is God. Here the claim is set forth that the one being dealt with is mind yet not a finite mind, and one who is capable of being known by direct contact. God is objectively real and independent of man's knowledge of him.[2]

The possibility of knowledge has various media by which it can become a reality. The claim to knowledge cannot be limited only to one method. Trueblood declares that one must maintain an "epistemological humility" or a "reverent agnosticism" toward the possibility of knowledge. A defensible agnosticism of one who is willing to listen and learn is better than a rigid dogmatism.[3] The type of agnosticism that affirms the impossibility of knowledge is, he states, advocating a self-contradictory position. "To establish complete skepticism a man would have to be omniscient, for we cannot know that nothing can be known unless we already know everything."[4]

Baillie's concept of religious knowledge will be approached with the presupposition that knowledge is possible in general and religious knowledge is possible in particular.[5] This presupposition is stated because it is beyond the scope of this work to prove that knowledge is possible. That would involve an altogether different study in itself. It has been indicated above that the best philosophical and theological minds of the ages have sought to establish the possibility of knowledge. That their conclusions have not been accepted by all need not necessarily cause misgivings. But that man is able to know in some way seems clearly discernible. If on no other grounds, the writer predicates the possibility of knowledge on his own self-conscious awareness of his present and immediate past thoughts. A. N. Whitehead has expressed this point with exactness in the following statement:

> In human experience, the most compelling example of non-sensuous perception is our knowledge of our own immediate past. I am not referring to our memories of a day past, or an hour past, or of a minute past. Such memories are blurred and confused by the intervening occasions of our personal existence. But our immediate past is constituted by that occasion, or by that group of fused occasions, which enters into experience devoid of any perceptible medium intervening between it and the present immediate fact. Roughly speaking, it is that portion of our past lying between a tenth of a second and half a second ago. It is gone, and yet it is here. It is our indubitable self, the foundation of our present existence.[6]

Knowledge and certitude. Baillie himself begins with the presupposition that man is a knowing subject. He does not attempt to prove that knowledge is possible. He answers that this in reality is true. He believes that knowledge connotes complete assurance. Knowledge implies certitude. But the certitude of knowledge does not exclude the possibility of knowledge of probabilities. To be certain of a probability, Baillie states, is not contradictory. He illustrates this by observing that of the next thousand babies born in Edinburgh some will probably be male and some female. Some of the seeds that he has planted in his garden are likely to germinate; or if a hundred men are asked a question, some will probably be more truthful than others. Although he acknowledges that the knowledge of probabilities is limited, he affirms that this probable knowledge does imply some certain knowledge. If this were not actually the case, then most of the natural sciences would have to be excluded altogether from the realm of knowledge because the most that can be claimed for any scientific result is a high degree of probability.[7]

Baillie is aware that there are different degrees or levels of knowledge. He believes that there is a difference in "knowing something less well" and "knowing it better." Although one may not know someone or something well, this does not connote a lack of all knowledge.8

Baillie follows the thought of J. H. Newman in making a distinction in usage between certitude and certainty. Certitude is concerned with the state of mind of the knowing subject. Certainty is the usage applied to the propositions which the knowing subject proclaims. To Baillie, neither of these usages has any meaning apart from a reference to the knowing subject. There is such an assurance in certitude for the inquiring subject that no room is left for doubt. Certainty will be entailed regarding propositions when they are predicated upon such evidence that would make doubting them an impossibility. The realities which confront the inquiring mind are "neither certain nor uncertain; they simply are."9

Real and putative knowledge. A distinction is made by Baillie between assured knowledge and putative knowledge. He declares that "to opine is not to know."10 He rejects the views of Greek thinkers like the Sophists and the logical positivist, Alfred Jules Ayer, who disclaim any real certainty in knowledge. Although the Christian is aware that his knowledge is restricted both in extent and in kind, he is, nevertheless, aware that he knows something even if it be limited. Since man is not a completely integrated personality or sinless, his opinions cannot be always equated with truth.

> We must also remember that there is a difference between knowing, and knowing that we know; or, what is the same thing, a difference between knowing that we know (or do not know) and merely thinking or opining that we know (or do not know).11

There is then no indefectibility in human thinking. Man always knows more and less than he is aware of. Man's intellectual honesty or his intellectual indolence prevent him from having an assured conviction of the truth. Since man is not infallible, he cannot claim to transmit the divine revelation in an infallible manner. Divine revelation as it issues from God is infallible, but in man's reception of it and transmission of it the human element is always involved and, therefore, any claim to infallibility must be disallowed. A distinction must always be made, then, between the divine revelation itself or the real knowledge itself and that which is communicated or opined about the truth. Real knowledge must be differentiated from putative knowledge if truth is to be realized.12

The limitations of knowledge. Man's knowledge will always suffer certain limitations because man is finite. Baillie does not believe, however, that man's finitude will disallow him from having any certitude in his knowledge. All authentic experience is transfused with certitude, but it is never possible for man to distil this certitude into the affirmation he makes concerning this reality. There is always the possibility of error when man begins to put into theoretical terms the reality which he has experienced.[13]

In the area of science, no results are regarded as final, but they are always subject to continuous correction and formulation. But there is always an element of certain knowledge in natural science, or else there could be no progress. Although there is always revision in the probabilities of science, the advance over the last conclusions indicates a move closer to the indubitable truth which science is seeking to discover. In the area of morality the same is true. While there is a sense of unconditional obligation, the attempt to distil this sense of obligation into specific moral rules becomes difficult. The obligation is absolute, but the attempt to codify this obligation is always to some degree provisional. Baillie believes that this same truth is also true concerning man's religious convictions. The Christian has authentic contact with ultimate reality and absolute truth, but his theological formulation of this reality can never be absolute or irreformable. His theological affirmations are always subject to correction, revision, and development. The Christian, then, can only speak of the ultimate in a dialectical manner. The element of paradox can never be fully excluded from man's theological formulation. This will always characterize the "finite reflection on the infinite."[14]

> It is for such reasons that, instead of claiming certainty or finality for our particular thoughts about God and the unseen world, I must content myself with claiming that certainty "pulsates through all our thinking" or that our experience in this realm is everywhere "transfused with certainty."[15]

II. KINDS OF KNOWLEDGE

Central to Baillie's whole concept of knowledge is the distinction which he makes between two kinds of knowledge: the knowledge of truth and the knowledge of reality. In this distinction he has attempted to elucidate what he considers the primary and secondary elements in knowledge. This distinction is carried forward in all his works. A difference is always maintained between the reality itself which is being ascertained and the formulations concerning the reality.

Knowledge of truth. The knowledge of truth with which Baillie is concerned here is not the exalted usage which makes it equivalent to reality but with the knowledge of truths or propositions. This is the distinction between knowing X and knowing that X is Y. In German and French there are separate verbs to distinguish two different aspects of "to know." The French use connaitre and savoir; whereas the Germans use kennen and wissen. Since English only has one verb to denote "to know," a distinction has to be made in other ways. Baillie follows the distinction made by Bertrand Russell between knowledge by acquaintance and knowledge by description. Knowledge by acquaintance is an awareness of reality in terms of immediacy; knowledge by description is concerned with the propositions or truths which are found to delineate the immediate reality which is known by personal acquaintance. In Baillie's opinion, man cannot be confronted with any reality without his mind beginning to form propositions about it; but he is convinced that it is the reality itself rather than the propositional truths about it which is the primary and immediate object of man's knowledge.[16]

Knowledge of reality. Baillie believes that man is able to have knowledge of reality. He disagrees with the Platonic view that the world perceived by the sense is not reality but only appearance. He affirms that the world of things seen is real. The reality that is seen, however, is not ultimate but only proximate reality. The world of things seen is created as distinct from uncreated reality. Baillie's distinction is not that of Greek thought which differentiates between the apparent and the real; but is, instead, the Christian discernment between the created and the uncreated.[17]

To Baillie, there are degrees of reality. This, he says, becomes apparent when one acknowledges, as he has done, that there is a distinction between realities that are not ultimate and ultimate reality. In discussing the derivation of the word, "reality," he observes that its source is rooted in a Latin word which means "thing" or "object." A better derivative could have been found, he believes, if the verb, "to be," had been relied upon as the Greeks did. Then reality would be concerned with being or that which is. Reality that is not ultimate also contains some unreality or non-being. This combination of being and non-being denotes man's finitude.[18]

The test of reality is presented by Baillie in the following manner:

> The test of reality (which is the same as to say of being or of objectivity) is the resistance it offers to the otherwise uninhibited course of my own thinking, desiring and

acting. Reality is what I "come up against," what takes me by surprise, the other-than-myself which pulls me up and obliges me to reckon with it and adjust myself to it because it will not consent simply to adjust itself to me.[19]

Reality always presents itself to man in the present and never in the past or the future. The past was once real, and the future may be real, but one's concern is with reality in the present. The realities of which man is aware are the external world, one's own self, his fellow man, and God. These realities are known directly by acquaintance and not merely by description.[20] Knowledge by acquaintance to Baillie entails a knowledge of persons. "To my mind knowledge of persons is the very type and pattern of what we mean by knowledge."[21] Personal knowledge is the most intimate and direct knowledge that man has. Even the reality of the natural world is apprehended by man not in isolation from the reality of other persons but as a world common to one's self and his fellow man. Baillie thinks that all existence is, in a sense, co-existence; because the reality of the natural world is in some means a derivative from the sense which one has of the reality of others. Man's physical experiences acquire objectivity through a prior recognition of the presence of other minds. Baillie seeks to repudiate the older epistemology that held that the only knowledge one could have was a knowledge of the external world and that one's self-consciousness and consciousness of others is dependent on and secondary to this knowledge. He is not satisfied with inferential knowledge when direct knowledge is possible. The plausibility of this position is held to be untenable on three grounds. First, self-consciousness does not arise before the recognition of others. Second, the consciousness of the external world does not precede such recognition. Third, even if the first and second possibilities were true, the recognition of other selves could not emerge from them.[22]

Human personality finds its real meaning only as the "I" is in relation to the "Thou." Man begins as a social being in community and then acquires solitude and not vice versa. All the objects of man's knowledge, his selfhood, the world of things, his fellow man, and God, are always presented in conjunction with one another. One of the objects is never known except in conjunction with the others.[23]

Baillie does not state that inference has no part in knowledge. He recognizes a two-fold aspect which it contributes to knowledge. First, an inferential element in knowledge is necessary if one is to identify a particular self as a self. Second, an inferential element is necessary in order to guide one in his interpretation of the character of others as he observes their bodily behavior and listens to them speak.24 What Baillie is striving for is not "the exclusion of an inferential element but the inclusion of an element that is not inferential."25 He believes the non-inferential element may be recognized in two ways. First, the reality of the existence of other minds does not arise originally as the result of inferential means. Second, the non-inferential element which is present in man by birth and rooted in his social experience must be allowed an essential role throughout the subsequent course of man's life. This will denote throughout the whole of man's life that there is an element of immediacy in all of one's knowledge of others. The intuitive and the discursive elements are intermingled. But the element of direct acquaintance is primary and the discursive element is secondary.26

Although Baillie is aware that man's knowledge is inadequate to describe the realities, and especially ultimate reality, he is convinced that man can have a real degree of certitude in his knowledge.

> Instead therefore of saying that we have no knowledge of realities but only of the judgements we make about these realities, we must say that our knowledge of the realities themselves--whether these be the external world or our fellow men or God--is primary, and our knowledge of truths concerning them secondary. The point, then, that I am most concerned to make is that, however difficult we may find it to ascribe certainty to these truths, we may nevertheless enjoy the certitude of having authentic acquaintance with the realities they fallibly seek to describe.27

III. IS RELIGIOUS KNOWLEDGE POSSIBLE?

If one allows the possibility of knowledge in general, then he should be willing to allow the possibility of religious knowledge in particular, although one might be unwilling to affirm its actuality. If one allows the possibility of the knowledge of realities, and if God is a reality, then he also can be known. Baillie believes that there is nothing of which man has a greater desire to have certitude about than the reality of God. God is not merely one reality among others to be known; but he is ultimate reality itself.

To Baillie, religious knowledge is possible because man is able to commune directly with God. God is envisioned as the prime reality who is known not by inference from something else already known, but who is the ground of man's knowledge of other things.28 When Samuel Johnson thought to refute Berkeley's apparent subjectivism, he decided not to try to prove the existence of such things as sticks and stones, but, instead, said he would bump the doubter's head against one of them and then he would know about this reality not by argument but by direct confrontation.[29] It is by direct confrontation with ultimate reality that Baillie believes man is aware of God's presence. "The position I am maintaining is that there is no reality by which we are more directly confronted than we are by the Living God."[30]

Rufus M. Jones has observed that it should not be considered so extraordinary that man is able to commune with God. Man's kinship is more closely in accord with God than with material things.

> If God is Spirit and man is spirit it is not strange, absurd or improbable that there should be communion and correspondence between them. The odd thing is that we have correspondence with a world of matter, not that we have correspondence with a world of spiritual reality like our own inner nature. The thing that needs explanation is how we have commerce with rocks and hills and sky. It seems natural that we should have commerce with That which is most like ourselves.[31]

Empirical knowledge. The philosophy of linguistic analysis has presented a sev re challenge to contemporary theological thought. The logical positivists claim that no knowledge can be accepted as true unless it is capable of verification in terms of sense experience. The empiricists aver that this makes the religious claim to knowledge of God meaningless because theological affirmations cannot be verified in terms of sense experience.[32]

When the empiricists claim that there can be no knowledge except that which is established on the evidence of bodily sense, Baillie argues that they are saying either that man can have no knowledge of any reality unless it is corporeal in nature, or that any non-corporeal knowledge of reality is established by observation of the corporeal. Since the empiricists today hold that the only direct knowledge one has is his own bodily selfhood, Baillie concludes, then, that analogy is impossible, because inference cannot be made from non-corporeal existence. "Since all reality is corporeal, the knower is as corporeal as the things he knows. But how can body know body? Only if knowledge is itself body."[33]

Baillie does not believe that everything can be judged on the same level. He, therefore, does not think that man's religious knowledge can be checked by reference to sense experience. Everything must be judged on the level of the experience out of which it arose.

> Our knowledge of other mind is therefore, like our knowledge of tridimensional space and all other primary modes of knowledge, something that cannot be imagined by one who does not already possess it, since it cannot be described to him in terms of anything else than itself.[34]

<u>Non-sensuous perception.</u> In Baillie's opinion, the empiricist has too narrowly limited the reference to veridical knowledge when it is reduced to bodily experience. Baillie's contention is that there is a "sense" experience of things other than the corporeal. "The human spirit, I shall say, develops certain subtler senses or sensitivities which go beyond the bodily senses."[35] He refers to the "illative sense," a sense of duty, a sense of beauty, a sense of humor, a sense of honor, a sense of the holy, and a sense of the presence of God. These "senses" presuppose the experience acquired through bodily senses, but, yet, go beyond the corporeal sense and bring an awareness of aspects of reality which could not be experienced otherwise. This sense is not based on argument but enables one to perceive something not otherwise perceptible. In this "sense" of the divine of which Baillie speaks, a cognitive element is present as well as a perceptional which disallows this sense from being reduced to a mere emotion or feeling.[36] It is a non-sensuous intuition of the divine. This sense of the presence of God is what Baillie denotes as the "non-sensuous perception."[37]

Man is directly aware of the divine presence. Faith is not based on a deduction or an inference from other realities but is a primary mode of awareness. But in all of Baillie's discussion about the sense of the presence of God, the act of perceiving is given greater emphasis although the act of conceiving is latently contained in all commitment.

The distinction is made that the non-sensuous perception itself is primary and the propositions describing that experience are secondary.[38]

<u>The ground of all knowledge.</u> God is the ground of all knowledge. "There is a sense in which all valid knowledge, all apprehended truth may be regarded as revealed."[39] In Baillie's opinion, no true knowledge ever begins from the human end whether it is concerned with the "number of peas in a pod" or the reality of God. Man's cognition is valid only as it is ascertained in relation to the reality by which he is confronted. When the reality that confronts man is God, the theological usage that distinguishes this relationship is always deeply mysterious, and no description of this encounter can ever be exhaustive.[40]

Although God is acknowledged as the ultimate ground of man's knowledge, Baillie is aware that man has no knowledge of what is at the divine end except that which is revealed to him through the relationship itself.[41] Any knowledge that man has of God comes through the activity of God's own spirit and not through the "unaided" exercise of man's intelligence. "What is true in any religious system is from God; what is false is of our own imagining. Man can know nothing of God except as God himself reveals himself to him"[42]

While God is the ultimate ground of all knowledge, this does not mean that all knowledge is knowledge of God. This view, Baillie states, would take all meaning out of the term revelation. Revelation and human discovery are not synonymous terms. Revelation and reason are not put in contrast to each other, however. From the divine side God's revelation is solely his activity, but man uses his rational faculty to grasp the revelation. Baillie contends that revelation and reason are not incompatible but go together at all times. God's disclosure comes to a rational creature who has the capacity to receive this revelation. While all knowledge has the potential of religious insight, the character of God's revelation is altogether different from the rest of knowledge.[43] In religious knowledge the initiative is always with God, who is the ultimate source and ground of all genuine knowledge.

CHAPTER II

GENERAL KNOWLEDGE OF GOD

Georgia Harkness is certainly correct when she observes that "there is no simple, clear, universally agreed-upon definition of revelation."[1] Understanding what is meant by revelation is, of course, the determining factor in arriving at a solution to the dilemma concerning revelation. In this section Baillie's epistemology will be examined to determine his understanding of the general knowledge of God.

I. THE NATURE OF RELIGIOUS KNOWLEDGE

General and special. This chapter has been entitled "General Knowledge of God" since a distinction between general knowledge and special knowledge of God was believed necessary in order to realize the full import of Baillie's view of religious knowledge. In Baillie's understanding, the nature of revelation is interpreted as a bifocal aspect of experience. From the human side man is led to a discovery of divine truth through the function of moral consciousness. The divine side of revelation is understood as essentially the self-disclosure of the spirit of God to man. Although this process may be described as bifocal, throughout Baillie's thought, the initiative in revelation always resides on the divine side.[2] General and special revelation are not seen as being bifurcated into two separate spheres, but are understood to be two varieties of revealed knowledge.[3]

The use of the terms general and special is deliberate since this usage will avoid, in the writer's opinion, the arbitrary and misleading distinction which is made in the use of the terms natural and revealed knowledge. It seems improper to speak of a natural knowledge of God since this would imply that the initiative is with nature itself instead of its creator. General revelation must be understood not so much as man discovering what he can from nature about God, but that everything, even nature itself, has the possibility of being used by God as a medium through which he reveals himself.

The terms general and special knowledge of God are preferred by Baillie to the traditional distinction which is made between a natural knowledge and a revealed knowledge, since he believes that general and special knowledge are really two varieties of revealed knowledge.[4] Baillie states in his Gifford Lectures that although he prefers the distinction between a general and special revelation to the traditional one between a natural and revealed knowledge, he does not find it completely satisfactory. He believes that there is something special in all revelation imparted by God.[5]

A solution to this problem can never be reached until the genuinely revealed aspects of all faiths are realized simultaneously with the distinctive features of Christianity. This will entail an admission to the reality of a revelation of God to all men of all nations. The nature of the knowledge of God can be rightly understood, then, only from a perspective which will allow, in at least some degree, for the legitimate reality of a revelation of God which is both general and special.

<u>Universality</u> <u>of</u> <u>religious</u> <u>knowledge</u>. In the opinion of the late Principal of New College, Edinburgh, there is a universality of religious knowledge among all races at all times.[6] He believes that "at least the <u>idea</u> of revelation is present in all cultures and in all religions."[7] He has clearly indicated his belief that all men have been made aware of God's presence to some degree and that none have ever been completely devoid of his revelation. In discussing Romans 3:1f, Baillie observes that "this means that the heathen as well as the Jews have been the recipients of some sort of revelation."[8] This view is acknowledged clearly in his Gifford Lectures: "Thus it is not only to Israel that God revealed himself through their successive historical experiences, but also to other peoples through theirs."[9]

Baillie understands genuine religious insight from any variety of religious traditions as having its ultimate source in God. From the crude expression of the savage to the full consummation of religious knowledge in the soul of Jesus, Baillie sees religion in its universality and breath of expression.[10] Christianity is interpreted by him not as a special aspect of religion, but as "religion itself." Christianity is depicted as "just religion itself, religion at its best and at its widest, faith in God at its surest and clearest."[11] Believing that all true religion is one religion, he states that the significance of Christianity resides "not so much in its uniqueness as in its universality, not so much in its originality as in its inclusiveness."[12]

It should be reiterated here that Baillie does not rely on the distinction between natural and revealed knowledge, but emphasizes instead that general and special revelation are two varieties of revealed knowledge. Emil Brunner also argues that general and special revelation are two varieties of revealed knowledge. Baillie maintains that this distinction is a remarkable gain that Brunner's view of revelation has over Karl Barth's concept.[13] However, in discussing Brunner's distinction between general and special revelation instead of the traditional distinction between natural and revealed religion, Baillie acknowledges that this is a change in the right direction, but notes that he is anxious to make a protest against this view when it depicts God as having provided the initial endowment in creation, but then God is pictured as having abandoned all the nations outside Israel without any further divine guidance throughout their remaining historical development.[14] Baillie believes that one must affirm that God is continuously involved in the affairs of all men in all ages and that any measure of true insight into "things divine," no matter how limited, that is found within the ethnic systems of religion has come about not by any accomplishment of man's exercise of his "unaided" reason, but from the activity of the spirit of God.[15] God has been actively engaged in the successive historical development of all mankind and not of Israel alone, revealing himself and seeking man's response.[16]

> What is true in any religious system is from God; what is false is of our own imagining. Man can know nothing of God except as God himself reveals himself to him. No man can by searching find out God, except as God himself takes the initiative both in prompting the searching and in directing the finding.[17]

Religious awareness. In contrast to the Barthian school of thought which claims that the only knowledge of God man has is derived from the special revelation in Jesus Christ, Baillie contends that all of humanity, however savage and backward it may be, has been confronted with the reality of God's presence.[18] He acknowledges that it may be questionable whether all men are aware of God as being a personal being, but he believes:

> It is not disputed that all peoples have such an awareness of the divine as is sufficient to awaken in them what it is impossible to regard otherwise than as a typically religious response.[19]

From the beginning God has been seeking out man, and man has never been left alone without some light from God. Baillie quotes from Plato, the Stoics, Cicero, Paul, and many others to show that man has never been devoid of all religious awareness of God, and, therefore, no one can plead total ignorance as an excuse for his sins.[20]

All the knowledge of God that man has is a result of the divine initiative in disclosing himself to man.[21] This divine self-disclosure is always from subject to subject,[22] and any true religious insight in any religion has come only from the activity of the spirit of God and not from the "unaided" exercise of human reasoning. Even the revelation that those outside Israel might have received has come about by divine initiative and not by man's inquiry.[23] "Man can know nothing of God except as God himself reveals himself to him."[24]

Following the Kantian philosophy, Baillie believes that man's moral values provide a category of religious awareness through which God is revealed. The *imago dei* is the moral consciousness which provides the focal point for divine revelation.[25] Man's sense of values is not something that he himself has acquired by his own strength but belongs to the progressive disclosure of the higher order of ultimate reality.[26] Baillie, therefore, surpasses the Kantian categorical imperative by stressing that the moral consciousness refers to a living person and not merely to an impersonal moral law. Absolute obligation can only be derived from the Absolute.[27] He argues that the source of the moral obligation is God himself who is directly revealed.

> Hence it is no mere law that is revealed to us, but a living Person, and what we call the moral law is but an abstraction which our limited and limiting minds make from the concreteness of the living Glory that is revealed.[28]

No allowance for the possibility that man's knowledge of God might arise from his subconscious level is conceded. It is never on the subconscious level that God enters into human experience but in the ethical realm of decision and response. Religious consciousness is not a result of the immediate contact of the subconscious mind with God; but the revelation of the divine presence arises in the fullest light of human intelligence on the ethical level rather than in a dim, instinctive, semi-cerebral psychosis.[29] Thus, Baillie would reject any attempt to relegate man's awareness of the reality of God to a subconscious level.

<u>Nature of man.</u> Baillie contends that the only humanity known is a humanity which has already been confronted and challenged by the reality of God's presence. Man has never been left alone by God, and he has been seeking man from the beginning. God has always been seeking to reveal himself to man, and a part of man's confession of sin is his awareness that he has possessed more light from God than he has used. Barth would emphatically differ with Baillie here and would maintain that no knowledge of God exists in the world except that which is in regenerate Christian believers. It is only through the revelation in Jesus Christ that Barth acknowledges a knowledge of God. Baillie believes that Barth makes no allowance for a point of contact or connection between the Christian gospel

and human nature.30 Baillie's criticism is justified in the light of the earlier writings of Barth, but it needs to be corrected to be in accord with Barth's revised view.

Barth's theology has presented a severe criticism of the "neo-Protestant bourgeois synthesis" which was achieved by liberal theology, and he has confronted this type of emphasis with a <u>Kerygmatic</u> theology which has presented the eternal Christian message over against the human situation. Having come through the liberal theological framework, Barth watched it collapse around him as the First World War brought an end to man's optimism about his own achievements. He also felt the inadequacy of its message when he stood before his congregation to preach. Barth felt that man was experiencing a "day of crisis" because man had ignored the gulf between himself and God. He believed that this crisis was only a symptom of the eternal crisis that man experiences when he is confronted by the living God. God confronts man in judgment, and man needs to realize the discontinuity between himself and God. Barth stated that liberal theology was wrong in thinking that man by his use of reason, natural theology, and mystical experience could arrive at a knowledge of God. He also deplored the optimistic view of man that was held by liberalism. In its place he sought to show man that he needed to come to the "crisis" in which he realized his helplessness and sinfulness. Because of the discontinuity between sinful man and the Holy God, the chasm can only be crossed by God. Salvation is God's action, not man's.31

Baillie does agree with many of Barth's criticisms of liberalism, as he too came through this same period and even had some of the same German professors as Barth did,32 but Barth's unwillingness to see within natural man himself anything which could in reality be the point of contact has been one of the decisive places where Baillie has differed with him. Baillie has insisted that all men have an awareness of God regardless of their locality and that there is within every man a point of contact with the ultimate. Barth has emphatically contended that there is no knowledge of God except in the heart of regenerate Christian believers. Barth stands in the tradition of Martin Luther, Albrecht Ritschl, and Wilhelm Herrmann in emphasizing a Christocentrism which states that Christ is the mediator not only of salvation but of the knowledge of God. Barth's theology is grounded upon Christology. He has said very plainly that "only the man who knows about Jesus Christ knows anything at all about revelation,"33 therefore, "the confession becomes inevitable that Jesus Christ <u>alone</u> is the revelation."34

Barth ultimately conceives the Word of God to be the Incarnation of the Eternal Word. God has revealed himself in the Word become flesh.

Through the use of mathematical figures, Barth has tried to throw some light on the question of revelation. Jesus Christ is the sheer perpendicular from above, coming plumb down to touch the world as a tangent at this single point. In another figure, Jesus Christ is pictured as the one in whom two planes intersect; one is known, and the other is unknown. The point on the line at which the relation between God and man becomes observable is in Jesus of Nazareth.[35] This single point is the most definite point because "the years A.D. 1-30 are the era of revelation and disclosure."[36] Here the coming of the Word took place once and for all in an historical occurrence and marks the point where the unknown world cuts the known world. In his Church Dogmatics, Barth declares: "At the climax of the Biblical witness the answer is to the effect that Jesus of Nazareth is the Lord. . . . He is the self-revealing God."[37] In another place he says: "God as our Father, as the Creator is unknown, in so far as He is not made known through Jesus."[38] In Barth's opinion, it is only through Jesus Christ that the revelation of God is made evident.

Baillie is convinced that Barth has "unduly simplified" the complexity of the spiritual situation which exists between God and man. Basing his interpretation on Barth's earlier writings, Baillie avers that Barth not only denies that there is any revelation of God apart from the Incarnation, but also denies that there is any point of contact or connection within natural man to which the Christian gospel can address its appeal. Baillie observes that Barth will not allow anything within man to serve as a point of contact to which revelation can link itself. He believes that the capacity to receive the revelation is given in and with the revelation itself. This view, Baillie asserts, is in a real sense a creation de novo.

Imago dei. To affirm that the imago dei has been so totally defaced as to leave no trace is unrealistic. The imago dei is understood, Baillie reasons, not as a doctrine derived from any knowledge of what happened at creation, but derived from man's knowledge of the present situation.[39] "The doctrine of the imago dei has its basis in the fact that our existent human nature presents itself to us, not as a simply bad thing, but as a good thing spoiled."[40] Baillie is willing to acknowledge that the imago dei has been "spoiled" or defaced, but he will not agree that it has been obliterated. He is convinced that all men have some awareness of God's reality.[41] In Baillie's opinion, Barth has obliterated the theological distinction between the creative and the redemptive activity of God. By his omnipotent power, God is creator, but the recreation of the imago dei in man is God's gracious activity. Barth's view is clearly that of two sheer omnipotent creations. If this were in fact the case, then God could, if he wanted to, create the capacity to receive revelation in a tree, or a stone as well as a man. As Baillie has so accurately observed: "Yet if it be true that man was first created in the image and likeness of God, the total obliteration of that image could mean only the total obliteration of his humanity."[42] It is Baillie's belief that the imago dei is not "wholly defaced or His voice wholly silenced" in anyone.[43] The only way God could have given man dominion over nature was to create him in his own image. The creation of the imago dei within man was God's way of endowing man "with some measure of what He Himself possessed in perfection, namely, intelligence, self-knowledge and the ability to 'look before and after.'"[44] The fact that man has been created in the image of God is the reason that it is possible for him to have communion with God.[45]

Baillie's contention is that the imago dei has its basis in the fact that our human nature presents itself to us as a good thing spoiled, and that the imago dei is the point of contact in human nature for the reception of God's revelation. This still allows man a free choice in the matter and also denotes that while God's gracious activity may be described as gratia praeveniens it can never be depicted as sheer omnipotence. There is always an element of self-limitation from the perspective of omnipotence since grace can be realized only "where there is free acceptance in the absence of all coercion."[46]

Baillie's discussion of Barth's concept of the imago dei, however, is noticeably dated in some respects. His chief criticism of Barth's view of the nature of man was written before some of Barth's changed perspectives were set forth in his Church Dogmatics and other writings. There seems to be little doubt that Barth's anthropology will not be completely satisfactory in spite of his new revision. He has noted his own dissatisfaction with it.[47] In his works, Barth has stressed the distinction between the natural man and the man of grace.[48] His earlier view depicts the image as being "totally lost."[49] In his latter works Barth states that man is created with a "covenant capacity" and this mode of man's existence cannot be destroyed by man's sin.[50]

Barth teaches that there is an ontological bond that unites every man to God. Although he believes that the imago dei has not been obliterated, he still argues that there is no point of contact in natural or fallen man. The point of contact is not found in man qua man. The point of contact in man is not his humanity or personality but is in the Word of God. The true imago dei is realized only in the man Jesus Christ. He is the "real man." Barth's concept of creation is grounded in his Christology. Man's relationship to God is by analogia relationis and not by analogia entis. Man's relationship with God is restored in Jesus, the "real man," who alone is man's unimpeded and unimpaired imago dei.[51] This is the reason, David L. Mueller believes, Barth does not retract his earlier polemic against natural theology.

> He answers that though there is an ontic continuity between Creator and creature, and though man as <u>imago Dei</u> remains such despite the fall, this cannot be known apart from faith in Jesus Christ.[52]

What Barth means by humanity is still not certain. He states that the humanity that is destined to relate to God is not humanity in general, but the specific humanity of Jesus Christ.[53] Since the only real man is Jesus Christ, men can become genuine men only as they are in a faith relationship with him. But this relationship involves a union of man with Christ to such an extent that man seems to be absorbed into the humanity of Christ to such a degree that it is universal and complete. Humanity itself is realized as a mode of God's own being.[54] Barth does note that the humanity of Christ is different from the rest of man, but his distinction here is not as clear as it needs to be to resolve the immense problems he has engendered.[55] Barth has moved from a position in which the <u>imago dei</u> in man was depicted as being "totally lost" to the position that man's humanity is absorbed into the projected humanity of God in Jesus Christ which ultimately destroys man's freedom as a real entity. Outside of a faith relationship in God, man is "totally lost," while within this relationship man is "totally absorbed." Barth's anthropology is still encumbered with many problems.

Emil Brunner's position on revelation has provided some common ground of agreement with Baillie on several points. Brunner has acknowledged the present reality of the <u>imago dei</u> as a point of contact and believes that God has given to all men in some degree a revelation of his presence.[56] Although Brunner believes that man is endowed with an intelligent and responsible personal nature, it is apparent that the receptivity and addressability of man's nature are merely the form or "empty frame" of the image of God. In Brunner's concept there is an absolute distinction between the form and the content of the image of God in man. The form is still intact, but the content of the <u>imago dei</u> is totally destroyed. He insists that man retains the complete form without any matter. Baillie argues that this is untenable. "That total wickedness," he declares, "is a self-destroying conception."[57]

Baillie shows the fallacy of Brunner's position in the following manner:

> What we are here asked to believe is that the form of rationality is still fully possessed by all men, while all have completely lost the power to do or to desire any-

thing good.

. . . .

> He does not see that if goodness were to cease to have <u>any</u> appeal to us, then our choice of the evil way would no longer be a <u>choice</u> at all, nor in any sense whatsoever the act of a free moral agent. The truth is that a totally corrupt being would be as incapable of sin as would a totally illogical being of fallacious argument. Evil, therefore, is essentially parasitic in nature, and not anything that exists, or could exist, in its own right, independently of God who is the Good. Evil feeds on the Good which it seeks to destroy, and in destroying it completely, would therefore destroy itself. It is thus in its very essence self-destructive. Hence total corruption is not anything that can exist but is, as has been said, a limiting conception which can be approached only asymptotically.[58]

The criticism of Barth and Brunner's position by Baillie is incisive in its logic, and Baillie's own position is much more realistic than that of either of these great thinkers. If God himself must create the <u>imago dei</u> afresh, then man is no higher than the nonrational animals below him. If man is absorbed into the humanity of God as projected in Jesus Christ, then he is not a responsible self, and his freedom and real significance are annihilated. Revelation is made to a rational, responsible being who is capable of response because of the rational power man has received in the creative process. The fact that this capacity has not been totally obliterated or totally absorbed is evident in the awareness of the reality of God to some extent in all men even today.

The meaning of the <u>imago dei</u> has been a matter of considerable debate. The <u>imago dei</u> has been interpreted to refer to the moral perfection of man, man's bodily form, man's dominion over nature and man's intelligence, among other things.[59] Whatever may be the final solution to this problem, it will arise, not from man's physical likeness to God which would seek to resolve the dilemma on the level of naive anthropomorphism, but will be realized only in the awareness of man's spiritual nature. The words ‏צֶלֶם‎ , "image,"[60] and ‏דְּמוּת‎ , "likeness,"[61] must refer to man's distinct relationship with God which is not shared by the lower creation. Man is depicted as having within him the "breath" or spirit of the living God himself.[62] This enables man to participate in the personal and spiritual fellowship with God. As S. R. Driver has stated:

"What is meant by the 'image of God'. . . It can be nothing but the gift of self-conscious reason, which is possessed by man, but by no other animal."[63] The _imago dei_ has been recognized as man's capacity for fellowship with God.[64]

The biblical account of the Fall is the dramatic presentation of the rupture of the intimate fellowship between God and man caused by man's sin. However, it is untrue to the biblical story and man's present nature as such to say that sin has totally defaced the image. Rad has observed that "the story of the Fall tells of grave disturbances in the creaturely nature of man," but he notes that the Old Testament has nothing explicit to say as to the way this affected the image of God in man.[65] Various other references in the Scriptures to the condition of man after the Fall denote the fact that the image has not been totally lost.[66] Man's religious consciousness has been perverted by his sinful rebellion, but the marred _imago dei_ is still man's point of contact with God who is seeking to address him.

Changed view. Noting that a changed view of revelation has occurred in which there is no longer an "old clear-cut distinction" between natural and revealed knowledge, Baillie states that a corresponding changed view of human nature has also taken place. Instead of revelation being absorbed into nature, nature has become engulfed in revelation. "Revelation, that is, has not come to be regarded as a more special kind of nature, but nature has come to be regarded as a more general kind of revelation."[67] In Baillie's opinion, human nature can no longer be regarded as a fixed endowment which God conferred on man at creation. He believes that human nature does not consist of various faculties which can be compartmentalized. Instead of being static and innate, human nature is interpreted as existing in a "state of becoming." Baillie rejects the Stoic view that the universality of belief in God arose from the soul of man. The Stoic thinkers have depicted man's soul as a detached part of the divine nature, and from this part certain innate ideas which constitute our moral and religious perspective have emerged. The influence of Berdyaev is apparent when Baillie states that "man without God is no longer man."[68] The humanistic approach which seeks to elevate man by his own self-importance is rejected. Human nature is considered empty and "sub-human" if it is not rooted in God. "The truth is that there is in man no _nature_ apart from _revelation._"[69]

> Our conclusion must therefore be that such moral and spiritual knowledge as may in any one period of human history seem to have become an inherent part of human nature, and so to be an "unaided" natural knowledge, is

actually the blessed fruit of God's personal and historical dealings with man's soul, and so in the last resort also a revealed knowledge.[70]

II. EPISTEMOLOGICAL STATUS OF NATURAL RELIGION

Involved in the examination of the epistemological status of what Baillie has called, "provisionally," natural religion is the problem of whether the pagan religions have any genuine knowledge of God and whether this knowledge, if genuine, arises from the natural realm itself or from another source. In the discussion above, it was abundantly evident that Baillie believed that not only Israel, but all men have been the recipients of revelation of God.[71] He rejects the traditional distinction between natural and revealed religion in favor of the distinction between general and special revelation. Although he believes this is a change in the right direction, he is anxious to affirm that "not all the light that God has imparted to the various pagan peoples in the course of their historical experience is general to them all; there is something that is special to each."[72]

<u>Nature as a medium of revelation.</u> Natural theology, as formulated by the Greek philosophers and carried forward by such Christian writers as Thomas Aquinas, is the attempt to arrive at the truth about God by speculative means based on a consideration of the natural world apart from historical religion. Baillie rejects both the tradition which has come down through Plato, Aristotle, and Aquinas that there are <u>sensibilia</u> within external nature from which man can deduce knowledge of God, and the Stoic position that there is a knowledge of God which is innate in human nature. Baillie prefers the Hebrew view which conceives of revelation as God's direct, personal covenant relationship with his creation. History is the realm in which God encounters man. If any men of any nation have knowledge of God, then it is from God himself for man cannot know anything of God unless God reveals himself to man. Thus, all knowledge of God is a result of revelation.[73] Nature in itself could only "half reveal" and "half conceal" God. God cannot be found in man's nature unless he is already within man's heart. If one looks at nature without the preparation of religious faith, it might appear severe and unrelenting.[74] The eye of faith is needed in order to discern the hand of the heavenly Father.[75]

In thinking about the revelatory aspect of nature, Baillie has observed that William Temple believes that either all existence is a medium of revelation or no particular revelation is possible.[76]

<u>Either all occurrences are in some degree revelation of God, or else there is no such revelation at all; for</u>

> the conditions of the possibility of any revelation require that there should be nothing which is not revelation.[77]

Baillie believes that Temple's position is not quite satisfactory. He acknowledges that the system of nature and its uniformity are an expression of the divine "will and wisdom." The attestation to this fact is noted in Psalm 19:1, and Romans 1:20, but he does not believe that a uniform sequence of natural events could, by itself, reveal God if he had not already revealed himself in a more personal manner.[78] He also observes that the nineteenth Psalm does not offer proofs of God to doubting minds, but spiritual nourishment to believers. "Certainly every religious man finds God present in nature; but that is only because he has already found Him present in his own soul."[79]

Nature is impersonal in itself, but God is personal, and his revelation is manifested in personal encounters with other persons.[80] Baillie follows the Kantian epistemology which limits scientific knowledge to the phenomenal world and makes natural science incompetent to formulate a basis for belief in God.[81] Nature, even in its mechanical uniformity, cannot be considered as a self-explanatory system. Thus, Baillie also follows more closely the Augustinian position, credo ut intelligam (I believe in order that I may understand), instead of the tradition of Aquinas or Calvin.

Baillie would tend also to follow more closely the Tillichian view rather than Temple's concept. Paul Tillich regards nothing as revelatory in its own right, but he believes that anything may become the medium of revelation.[82] Baillie qualifies this view by stating that he believes that "revelation is always given us through events"[83] and that the fullness of revelation can only be given in a personal way.[84] Thus, he declares that "the fullness of revelation is only in Jesus Christ, and in Him all other revelation is comprehended and summed up."[85]

Clifford Braman has criticized Baillie's repudiation of natural theology in the light of his acceptance of the reality of the imago dei. Braman declares that it seems inconsistent for Baillie to give the basis he does to man's ethical nature and at the same time to deny man the use of his rational faculty in arriving at a knowledge of God by an observation of nature.

> If the imago dei, in Baillie's view constitutes man both as an intelligent and ethical creature, it seems illogical to deny the possibility of natural theology while affirming the capacity of the moral consciousness for apprehending God.[86]

If Baillie's view is correctly understood, it would be illogical for him to hold any other position than the one he does. It is legitimate for Baillie to interpret the imago dei as the capacity within man which constitutes him as an intelligent and ethical creature, but his whole emphasis on the way God reveals himself to man places the stress on God's initiative and not on man's. The imago dei is the point of contact within man, but man by making an observation of the natural realm is not able to acquire a knowledge of God as personal. If God's revelation is always personal, then it is impossible for the natural realm in itself, which is impersonal, to disclose God to man. Baillie does not deny man's rational power, but he does deny that this faculty can by observation of nature arrive at genuine knowledge of God. The inconsistency lies in Braman's attempt to follow the tradition which would produce proofs of a personal God based on an impersonal natural realm. In speaking of man's consciousness of God, Baillie states that God's immediacy is given in conjunction with the consciousness of the corporeal world.

> We do not know God through the world, but we know Him with the world; and in knowing Him with the world, we know Him as its ground. Nature is not an argument for God, but it is a sacrament of Him.[87]

Nature and grace. Baillie states that in rejecting the doctrine of the total corruption of human nature he is at the same time rejecting the concept of a complete discontinuity between nature and grace. He believes that there is some continuity between the natural life and the spiritual, otherwise man could not respond to the revelation of God. A man in whom the imago dei has been totally effaced would no longer be a man. Baillie refuses to draw a sharp line of demarcation between grace and nature. Instead of an abrupt dichotomy between the two states, he alleges that no man is wholly outside of fellowship with God. Man would have to be totally corrupt to be out of fellowship with him. Any good within man arises from fellowship with the source of all good--God.[88] Baillie prefers a scale of forms or degrees rather than a distinct point below which one could say that grace does not extend.[89]

The following paragraph sets forth his view:

> It is thus possible to hold that the self-same image of God, which by the power of Christ is restored in the souls of the saints, is to be found dimly and brokenly reflected in all human nature, behind and below the ravaging defacements of sin's corruption; and at the same to magnify to the uttermost the implacably urgent need of the

restoration itself, of the new creation and the new birth.[90]

Baillie's view of nature and grace is in accord with his over-all view of revelation. Since there can be no knowledge of God without the initiative of God himself, any knowledge that man has of God comes only through personal fellowship. By rejecting a dualism between two distinct states of existence, Baillie affirms his allegiance to the principle of continuity. All men are dimly aware of God's presence even in their sin, otherwise response would be impossible if they were totally corrupt. This belief is also consistent with his view that in some sense all men believe in God in the "bottom of their hearts" even if they deny him with the "top of their minds." Although this view will be discussed at greater length in another chapter, a few words are appropriate here. No quarrel is intended with the view that in some sense an element of continuity must be acknowledged within man's nature if he is to respond to God. The question of man's freedom in respect to God's grace must be raised if the principle of continuity is to be correctly understood. If man, simply because he is man per se, is included within the gracious favor of God when he himself has chosen to rebel against this gracious activity, is this, then, not a denial of man's very freedom itself? In his concept of the imago dei, Baillie has stressed forcefully the element of freedom in man's nature. However, if man's freedom to respond is subdued by God's omnipotence is not man qua man totally defaced? Without freedom does man still maintain the imago dei? Is there any real choice if it is not personal, conscious and cognizant? It is apparent that the answer will have to be no.

III. HUMAN DISCOVERY AND DIVINE REVELATION

The relation of discovery and revelation. At the beginning of this chapter it was noted that Baillie's view of divine revelation could be understood as bifocal. From the human side man is led to a discovery of divine truth through the function of moral consciousness. Revelation, however, is viewed as essentially divine activity, the self-disclosure of God to man.[91] This is Baillie's way of trying to describe the communion between man and God. He does not believe that divine truth can be divided into a two source theory which would make a division of divine truth into that which may be discovered by human reason and that which must be accepted from divine revelation. Human discovery and divine revelation, when properly understood, are "complementary sides of the self-same fact of experience."[92] Revelation and reason are not alternatives appropriate to other areas, but are the divine and human sides in man's knowledge of God. All divine truth is grasped by man's use of his rational faculty as he responds to the divine revelation. Baillie believes that man has been created with intelligence which God means for man to use to discover all he can about nature.[93]

It needs to be observed here that although Baillie's view of revelation has been interpreted as bifocal this does not mean that he considers human discovery and divine revelation as two aspects of the same process in the sense that all truth is both discovered and revealed. This is not the case. To view revelation in this way would destroy all meaning in the concept of revelation.

> To say that God reveals Himself cannot mean merely that He exists to be known or that He is always there for men to discover if they can. His self-disclosure must mean something more active than this.[94]

It is not correct to claim, Baillie avers, that all knowledge is knowledge of God. He believes that there is present, in a potential sense, in all knowledge something akin to religious insight and thus ultimately is from God. However, it is not necessarily true that because our human knowledge is by discovery it is also revelation, and, therefore, all human knowledge is due to revelation. The truth is more clearly seen when it is realized that there is no knowledge totally unrelated to God's self-disclosure; but the knowledge that man understands as religious knowledge is of a different degree from the rest of his knowledge.[95]

The distinction between discovery and revelation. Ultimately no aspect of divine truth can be apprehended unless God himself shall make it known. Nevertheless, while aware that no human thought is independent of divine illumination, it is necessary to distinguish between revelation and discovery. Man's rational ability has been conferred on him by God's creative act. Man's rational faculty is a part of his total being which constitutes the imago dei. The total obliteration of this image could only mean the total obliteration of his humanity. This is the factor which sets him above the beasts. With his rational faculty, man is at liberty to discover all he can about the natural world in which he lives. The discoveries of science, medicine, education, and those in other media have all come about by the use of the rational faculty which God has given man as an inherent part of his nature. All of this knowledge of man is on the natural level, and any knowledge that man infers from this level will not of necessity be that which leads to absolute truth. It is possible through the eye of faith for man to know something about God from the natural realm, but this will not of necessity lead him to a religious experience with God. Man is aware that God is in some sense involved in the natural order because he is aware of his presence within his heart.

Man is able to discover whatever he can from the natural realm, but he is not able by inference to deduce proof from this realm that will result in personal encounter with God. This would be man's initiative and not God's. Man is not able by inference or argumentation to reach ultimate reality. General revelation is not able within itself to culminate in special revelation. The problem of evil is always the greatest inhibition against drawing inferences from the natural realm about God. Nels F. S. Ferre's conclusion seems to be correct when he observes that the problem is not simply one of epistemology but of ontology.

> It is a question not only of knowing but of being. God simply is not present <u>as</u> <u>personal</u> <u>love</u> in any flower, root and all! The sunset by itself reveals no living Father, the Lord of life and of eternity.[96]

The atheist is a witness to the fact of this truth. One cannot by a necessary or natural transaction advance from the realm of nature to that of ultimate reality. Through the eye of faith one can envision the order and beauty of the natural realm as evidences of the creative and sustaining power of the personal God of the universe, but God can never be equated with his creation <u>per</u> <u>se</u>. This is the fallacy of pantheism. Nor can man by his own initiative discover him there. Baillie's distinction between discovery and revelation, therefore, seems valid.

CHAPTER III

SPECIAL KNOWLEDGE OF GOD

Attention can now be directed to Baillie's view of the knowledge of God as it is manifested in special revelation. This is done with the understanding, as was noted in the last chapter, that to Baillie there is something special in all of God's revelation.[1] There has been no attempt to deny all extra-Christian revelation, but a specific acknowledgement has been made that God has revealed himself in some sense to all men through various media. The Judaeo-Christian tradition has affirmed that God himself has made his presence known in a special way through certain historical events, culminating uniquely in the Incarnation. This is the aspect of Baillie's thought which shall now be examined.

I. THE NATURE AND CONTENT OF REVELATION

In defining revelation, Baillie notes that it "literally means an unveiling," a disclosure of something that was formerly hidden. A distinction is made between disclosure and discovery. Disclosure carries with it the meaning of uncovering, but it does not ordinarily mean to discover. A discovery is made by someone, but a disclosure is made by one to another. All true knowledge is determined by the object and not the subject. No valid knowledge can be acquired except that which is already present either waiting to be known or seeking to be known. Attending, selecting, and interpreting are active functions of the knowing mind, but the mind must attend to, select from, and interpret that which is presented to it. The knowing mind must then not only be active in its response but passive as well.[2] In respect to God, Baillie believes that this same principle of knowing is also true. No true knowledge of God can be explained by beginning from the human side. The validity of man's cognition is determined by the reality which confronts him. The revelation which the Bible affirms is not of an object to a subject but from subject to subject. Revelation is always given within a personal relationship.[3] Baillie believes that this is not only true concerning the way of knowing, but it is also true concerning the content of knowledge. The divine self-disclosure is not only a disclosure from subject to subject but a disclosure of subject to subject. Revelation then is not information about God but the self-revelation of the Divine. Revelation is not concerned with propositional truths about God but with the personal encounter and personal communion with the living God himself.[4]

Divine Self-Disclosure

The central theme Baillie seeks to convey in most of his books, and especially in Our Knowledge of God, The Idea of Revelation in Recent Thought, and The Sense of the Presence of God, is that God is known by man not by argument but by his being directly confronted by the divine presence. "The position I am maintaining is that there is no reality by which we are more directly confronted than we are by the Living God."[5]

The tradition of natural theology. Baillie observes that the prevailing practice of the Western philosophy has been to regard the truthfulness of the existence of God as a conclusion which could be reached by the means of argument. This tradition, as he traces it, has its roots in ancient Greece; and Plato is considered the first to attempt to prove the existence of God by argument.[6] The phrase "proof of the existence of God" is first found in his works. This view is passed on by Aristotle and others until its influence is felt within Christian theological and philosophical thought of the Middle Ages. During the Middle Ages, Thomas Aquinas continues in a most influential manner the Aristotelian proofs for the existence of God.[7]

Aquinas is regarded by non-Catholic theologians and historians as the quintessence of the Scholastic spirit of the Middle Ages. The authority of Aquinas as the leading philosopher of the Roman Catholic Church was established officially by Pope Leo XIII in 1879 in the encyclical Aeterni Patris. The traditional orthodox Christian in the thirteenth century followed Augustine and the Neoplatonism that he had adopted. They had rejected Aristotle because of the corruption of his thought by Arabian interpretation, especially Averroism. Aquinas sought to show that when Aristotle was freed from this Arabian contamination there was revealed a philosophy which was sound in its principles and could be of invaluable service to Christian thought.

Differing with the Augustinians of his century, Aquinas held that an autonomous philosophy based upon experience and the insight of human intellect is possible. Although he modified Aristotle's teaching at many points, he accepted completely the Aristotelian view that sense-experience is the source of all human knowledge. At this point he was consistently Aristotelian when he stated that the origin of our knowledge is in sense, even of those things that are above sense.[8]

There were many differences between Plato and Aristotle, but one of the most significant differences for this study was epistemological. Plato had claimed that man had a faculty of direct vision by which he could see

God, while Aristotle insisted that all knowledge comes through the senses. In combining Aristotelianism and Christianity, Aquinas made a sharp distinction between natural and revealed theology. The synthesis that he made was most apparent in his natural theology. Here he brought the supernatural into organic relation with the natural. Natural theology, he stated, begins from the human end and ascends to the divine, while revealed theology begins from the divine side and descends to the human. Natural theology contains all the truth that can be discovered by the Aristotelian principle about God and man which can be deduced from sense-experience. Etienne Gilson, a contemporary interpreter of Aquinas, has observed two main classes which are distinguishable in Aquinas' concept of knowledge. The first class constitutes revealed truths such as the existence of God and his essential attributes which are acquired by reason alone although they are revealed. In answer to the question of what purpose is the necessity of revelation if man can attain this knowledge by his own reason, Aquinas replies that the truth must be revealed for those who do not have the cognitive ability and who must, therefore, respond in simple faith. The second class of revealed truths is composed of all the articles of faith which surpass the range of human reason such as the Trinity, the Incarnation and man's redemption. Reason cannot be used to prove these articles true, but neither can it be used to prove them false.[9]

Baillie, following more closely the Kantian view of knowledge, rejects the Aristotelian concept of the knowledge of God. He rejects Aquinas' view of the Scriptures which are regarded primarily as a body of communicated information, and he also rejects Aquinas' view of faith which is depicted as the acceptance of this communicated information by authority. Often Aquinas compares faith to a schoolboy's acceptance upon the word of his teacher certain facts for which he does not yet know the evidence. Baillie attempts to be fair to Aquinas' view by noting that faith to him is not only an intellectual process but is also a function of the will.[10] Baillie is convinced that Aquinas believed that those who have had training in philosophy were in a special class. For this class, logical argument becomes the only ground for their assurance of the reality of God's existence.[11]

The biblical tradition. In contrast to the tradition which seeks to establish the existence of God by argument, Baillie sets forth what he considers to be the older and more correct view. God's existence is assumed throughout the Old Testament. The knowledge of God denoted in the biblical record is founded on the direct revelation of God himself in specific events and not on cosmological speculation. The Old Testament, in Baillie's opinion, does not attempt to argue or prove that God exists, and, thus, the Old Testament writers did not attempt to argue what they already knew within their own consciousness.[12] Baillie finds this same emphasis within the New Testament. Jesus stressed that man's trouble does not lie in his non-belief in God. In the New Testament, unbelief was not an intellectual persuasion of God's non-existence. The men Jesus rebuked for their lack of faith were not men who denied God with their minds, but those who accepted him with their intellect yet lived as if he did not exist.[13]

> Thus for the New Testament, as for the Old, God is One who is directly known in His approach to the human soul. He is not an inference but a Presence . . . . . The knowledge of God of which the New Testament speaks is a knowledge for which the best argument were but a sorry substitute and to which it were but a superfluous addition. "He that hath seen me hath seen the Father; and how sayest thou then, Shew us the Father?"[14]

The influence of Greek philosophy. The real threat that Baillie directs against the traditional argumentation for God's existence is seen in his complete rejection of logical argument of any kind as the process by which God's reality is known. He challenges the tradition from Aquinas which says that man has no knowledge of God per se but only per ea quae facta sunt, through his effects in the natural world. He allies himself with the other tradition in medieval thought which is represented in Bonaventure's dictum that God is present to the soul itself. To those who have not been confronted by the reality of this presence, all argument is useless, and to those who have already had this experience it is superfluous.[15]

Because Baillie does not accept the Aristotelian view of revelation as set forth by the Medieval Synthesis, it does not mean that he depreciates altogether the contribution of Greek philosophy. In fact, Baillie is very appreciative and greatly influenced by Greek philosophy, especially Platonism. In an autobiographical sketch, he states that in a real sense he is a "Christian Platonist."[16] John A. Mackay makes mention of a doggerel which was scratched on a desk in Baillie's classroom: "Baillie, Baillie, give us your answer true. Why ain't Plato found in the canon, too?"[17] He observes that this may serve to describe the enthusiasm for Platonic thought which Baillie's students felt that he maintained throughout his teaching and which was evident in his writing.

In a paper read at the Conference of Theological Seminaries at Toronto, Canada, Baillie argues that the fusion of Greek rational criticism with the simple Galilean gospel was a necessary step. He realizes that certain weaknesses of the Greek tradition may have been absorbed into

Christian thought in the process, but he is convinced that Christianity would not have conquered the Graeco-Roman world if the absorption had not taken place. Baillie asserts that Christianity was born among the Jews but grew up among the Gentiles.[18]

In all of his writings, Baillie places a large stress on the rational and logical aspects of the Christian faith. His epistemological outlook, which has been influenced by the Augustinian and Kantian philosophies, will not allow him to accept the view which seeks to arrive at a genuine knowledge of God by inference from the natural realm. Knowledge of God's existence is not the result of an inference of any kind, but comes only through direct personal encounter with God.[19]

The true function of argument. Although Baillie does not believe that one can prove the existence of God or arrive at a knowledge of his reality by inferences from the natural realm, he does contend that there is a true function of argument with respect to the existence of God. A legitimate kind of theistic proof is to bring the belief to a consciousness of itself. In an Anselmic type formula, Baillie states: "For though we may not try to prove either to ourselves or to others that God exists, we may do something to persuade both ourselves and others _that we already believe in Him._"[20] This is the end toward which Baillie confesses that his book, _Our Knowledge of God_, has been directed.[21] Baillie states that his position is summarized in Pascal's words, "'Thou wouldst not be seeking me, hadst thou not already found me. Be not therefore disquieted.'"[22] Baillie's position is an expansion of Pascal's insight. The "true office of argument" is to lead men back to the point where they can again become self-conscious of the direct presence of God which has never really left them. Showing the Kantian influence upon his thinking, Baillie sets forth a type of "moral proof." The unconditional or absolute demand that confronts man in his consciousness of value contains in itself the recognition of the holy God who is its source. He sets forth two propositions in defense of this argument. "First, that _no obligation can be absolute which does not derive from the Absolute._"[23] Second, since morality is essentially a function of personality, there can be no moral obligation to an Absolute if the Absolute is not apprehended as personal.[24] This moral obligation to the Absolute is no mere submission to an alien authority. Baillie believes that it is only in a self-surrender to the Absolute that man realizes his highest good and perfect liberty.[25]

The "logic of religion," as Baillie understands it, is not derived from any source outside itself but is "latently contained within it." The believer is not to be furnished with new reasons for believing in God, but is to be led to a clearer consciousness of why he has always believed.[26]

This awareness is in man's consciousness of moral obligation. The only way this belief can be made more certain is in "the progressive deepening of the religious insight itself" and not in the pursuit of any independent scientific inquiry.[27]

Baillie himself seems willing to grant that there is some truthfulness contained in Anselm's argument which is valid, especially in the field of mathematics and the natural sciences. In geometry it is true that a conclusion is reached by a syllogistic process, but when it comes to religion, Baillie believes, it is on the other end of the scale from the field of knowledge of pure mathematics. Yet in religion it is not the rigour of logic, but the "practical acquaintance" with the ultimate reality from which our logical reasoning begins.[28]

Revelation and History

Historical. History is the medium through which God's revelation comes to man. Although Baillie believes that man is directly and intimately confronted with the presence of God, he insists that God's presence never comes to man in a vacuum, but always in conjunction with his knowledge of others and the corporeal world.[29] God may not be known through the world, but man is able to know him with the world and in knowing God in conjunction with the world, he is known as its ground. Knowledge of God also comes in conjunction with the knowledge of others. This means that religious individualism is rejected, and the need for the Church as the center of corporate fellowship is better understood. History is understood as the medium that enables man to have fellowship with God. Christianity is a historical religion. History has meaning only if it has a center. Christ is the center of history, and he, as the center, determines its beginning and conclusion. Christ is the center through which all history receives meaning.[30] "The Christian knowledge of God is not given to any save in conjunction with the telling of an 'old, old story.'"[31] History becomes a medium which makes it impossible for man to know God without being united to his fellow man. The meaningfulness of history is centered in the Incarnation and the cross. In revealing himself through the historical tradition, the past becomes relevant to a person now because God reveals himself through that medium in the present.[32]

Baillie does not believe that the whole of history in itself is revelatory. History as such is impersonal, just as nature is impersonal. Since God is personal, he can only reveal himself in a personal way. The Bible is concerned with history, but the chief actor in history is God not man.[33] History is a process of action and reaction between the external events and the human response to them. There is always the interaction of mind and event. The events in themselves are conditioned by the human experience.[34] Under the influence of C. H. Dodd, Baillie avers that history is always "events plus meaning." This he believes is true also of biblical history. The Hebrew concept of history is different from all other religious literature because it is "essentially a record and interpretation of events."[35] The Old Testament record of God's revelation is a story of divine action and human action. The initiative always comes from God, but his second move depends upon the response of men to his initial act. This interaction, Baillie states, is clearly seen when one comes to the New Testament.[36] In Jesus Christ the interaction of divine and human are discernible in the one who was "both very God and very man." It is in the Incarnation alone that revelation is perfected. "This intercourse of the divine and the human is the very meaning of the Incarnation."[37]

Revelation of God in Jesus Christ. The consummation of God's revelation in history is realized in the Incarnation. Baillie has stated that revelation is always given through events, yet only through those events that are God's mighty acts. These events become revelatory only to those who have apprehended their significance by the power of God's Spirit. The fullness of revelation can be understood only in a personal sense. In agreement with William Temple, Baillie states that since man is a person, he can understand only that which is personal, and since God is a personal being, he reveals himself in a personal way.[38]

The Incarnation of God in Jesus Christ is believed by Baillie to be the very essence of the Christian faith. "The fullness of revelation is only in Jesus Christ, and in Him all other revelation is comprehended and summed up."[39] In Jesus Christ the "very face of the Most High" has been revealed.[40] It was noted in the above section that Baillie sees the meaningfulness of history as being centered in the Incarnation and the cross. Christ is the pivotal point that gives history its meaning. "God was in Christ reconciling the world to himself"[41] is believed by Baillie to be the event upon which the Christian faith is founded. He believes that there is no question that the Incarnation is the central doctrine of the Christian faith.[42] He does not hesitate to speak of the "necessity of the cross,"[43] and of the "scandal of particularity."[44] The via dolorosa is seen as God's way to redeem man. At the center of the Christian religion stands a cross.[45]

God's revelation is not a passive process on his part. God has not been passively waiting to be discovered, and finally someone has succeeded in finding him in Jesus Christ. God did something in Christ for the redemption of man. "The Christian gospel is rather that in Christ

God _did_ something for the human race greater and more splendid than He had ever done before."[46] Although Baillie believes that the eternal mind and will have been fully revealed in Jesus Christ, he does not want to say that God is Incarnate in Jesus alone, but prefers to speak of God as being Incarnate "supremely" in Jesus.[47] In another place, he maintains that "we must indeed be careful not to think or speak as if Jesus Christ were the only man in whom God has ever revealed Himself at all."[48] Again he states that "revelation and incarnation are no unique historical prodigies but are, by God's grace, of the very warp and woof of our human experience."[49] God still continues to speak "at sundry times and in divers manners."

It is evident that many men have served as media through whom something of the revelation of God has been made known. To deny the uniqueness of the Incarnation in Christ in order to allow for a general revelation seems unnecessary and is tantamount to undermining the very foundation upon which the Christian faith is based. In Christ was truly revealed the "fullness" of God's revelation, and in Christ was truly revealed the unique person who was constituted by the Incarnation.

Although it is difficult to say with exactness, it appears that Baillie has modified his position somewhat in his later works. All the above quotations are from his earlier works, but even in one of the earlier works, he speaks of the "uniqueness and irreplaceableness of God's self-revealing" in Christ.[50] However, the "scandal of particularity," "the necessity of the cross," and "Christ as the center of history" are emphasized in his later works. In _Our Knowledge of God,_ he speaks of the necessity of Christ, God Incarnate in the flesh.[51] In his discussion of the condescension of God and the humility of Christ, he stresses the importance of acknowledging the "kind of man" that was involved in the Incarnation in order to understand the concept of "salvation in _this_ name." Here he certainly seems to be stressing a uniqueness about the nature of the Incarnate one.[52] In two articles published in _The International Review of Missions,_ he expresses renewed interest in the Incarnation.

> We must preach only Christ, we must be much more careful than we have been in the past that it is only Christ whom we preach, but we must preach Christ Incarnate in the whole life of man.[53]

In the other article, he speaks often of something that God has done in Jesus Christ for the human race "as He had never done before."[54] The _Kerygma_ is spoken of as a recital of events, events which are all part of a "single grand event" about something that happened in history at a "particular time."[55]

While Baillie is not clear in his discussion of the uniqueness of the Incarnational event, he does interpret it as the "fullness" of God's revelation to man.[56] Jesus is interpreted as the supreme man, the preeminent Son of Man, the greatest of all religious leaders. He was the greatest and best believer who ever lived.[57] He is the Church's "greatest saint" and is also her Lord.[58] Baillie does not believe that it is sufficient to claim that Jesus represented man's highest grasp of God; Jesus was also God's fullest revelation to man. In Christ God has spoken in the greatest revelation of himself.[59]

The crowning glory of the Christian religion is not mere talk or words but that the Word became flesh.[60] This is the event of which the New Testament speaks in John 1:14. The event of which the New Testament speaks is the personal Word. Baillie observes that in the Old Testament the most common phrase used to express revelation is "the word of Yahweh," which is mentioned about four hundred times. The word of Yahweh came to a prophet. In Baillie's opinion, the word, even as it came to the prophets, was not contrasted with the deed or speech contrasted with action as it was in Greek thought. "But in Hebrew the usual word for 'word' also means an action or an event, and 'for such thought God's fiat and his effective action are one.'"[61] Baillie points to several scriptural references for support.[62] The coming of Jesus Christ is the objectification in time of the eternal nature of the Logos. In the Incarnation of the Logos, the word has become uniquely historical.

Revelation and Mystery

Any concept of revelation involves the element of mystery. Since God is holy in nature, he is mysterious. Revelation is the lifting of an obscuring veil or the disclosing of something that has been hidden.[63] In his revelation, God's presence is always veiled. Although God is known directly, this confrontation is a mediated immediacy. Baillie uses Luther's figure of the Deus absconditus. God is never known in his "naked" majesty but only in a veiled form. Baillie believes that there is an immediacy about Luther's knowledge of God that is not found in the teachings of Aquinas. God reveals himself to man directly but in a veiled form. "In this sense the Deus revelatus is a Deus velatus, a Deus absconditus; the unveiled God is a veiled and hidden God."[64] This is Baillie's way of stating the mysterious nature of revelation. God never reveals himself without mystery. There would be no mystery without disclosure, but if God were fully disclosed, there would cease to be a mystery. Baillie quotes approvingly the following statement: "Revelation, therefore, is of the very nature of Deity. God is a self-disclosing Mystery."[65] What is disclosed in God's revelation is not a body of esoteric knowledge but the "mystery of the Kingdom." "It is the kingdom itself that is the mystery, and the kingdom is the presence or <u>Parousia</u> of God in Christ."[66]

II. THE RECEPTION OF REVELATION

No event can be spoken of as revelatory unless someone has apprehended the revelation. Baillie believes that an act of revelation is not complete until its reception has taken place. "The illumination of the receiving mind is a necessary condition of the divine self-disclosure."[67] There must be an intercourse of mind and event. The essence of revelation is realized in the guidance by God of both the event of revelation and the person who responds. In agreement with Brunner, Baillie declares that even Jesus Christ is not revelation of God until a response is made. Just as Christ would not be redeemer if there were no one for him to redeem, so revelation is incomplete without someone who is responsive. God's spirit directs both the response made by men to his divine revelation as well as the revelatory approach itself. God's illumination provides the inspiration to interpret the revelation. Inspiration, therefore, is the necessary counterpart to the concept of revelation.[68] God's revelatory events become meaningful as his spirit inspires men to respond to the divine claim made for them. God is active in the bifocal aspect of revelation. Man responds with the totality of his being to the God who is constantly seeking to make his presence known.

<u>Knowledge</u> <u>by</u> <u>encounter.</u> The chief emphasis in Baillie's concept of the reception of revelation is his stress on the direct encounter of man with the living God.[69] Man's knowledge of God comes as a result of direct, personal encounter with God and not by inference based on the natural realm or some other source. It is a personal experience with ultimate reality. Having rejected the view that reduces man's knowledge of God to sense experience, Baillie affirms his belief in the knowledge of God that comes by direct confrontation of God himself. Baillie has described this encounter in various ways: "the challenge of his holy presence," "the reality of God," "the living God," "the divine," "awareness of a divine reality," "the transcendent holiness of God," "the challenge of God in Christ," "the continual invasion of our life by his holy presence," "the divine self-disclosure," "the presence of God in Jesus Christ," "the sense of the presence of God," and "direct apprehension of reality."[70] His main emphasis throughout is on the directness and immediacy of the encounter. God is known in his direct approach not by inference but by the reality of his presence.[71]

From his earliest publications to his latest, Baillie has contended that man's knowledge of God is not by inference but by personal encounter. In The Interpretation of Religion he states:

> It is plain enough, then, that it was not as the result of an argument that faith first arose in the world and that it is not as the result of an argument that it normally arises in men's minds to this day.[72]

The only true religious argument for the being of God comes in actual personal communion with the divine.[73] Baillie is convinced that no argument can ever bring faith in God to birth within man. Mankind had belief in God long before it tried to give a clear reason for this belief. Men are not likely to be led to belief by a logical exposition of its grounds.

> I did not believe the proposition about the square of the hypotenuse until I was provided with the argument; but I believed in God long before I had heard of any of the arguments for His existence. If men begin by being without all belief in God, it would be quite hopeless to try to convert them by argument. Men will believe in God only when they find themselves unmistakably confronted by his holy presence.[74]

In his Gifford Lectures, Baillie maintains his repudiation of the approach which seeks to acquire a knowledge of God by inference. In his opinion, no knowledge has the certitude as that which is contained in direct, personal experience. Man's knowledge of God does not come by the "unaided" experience of human wisdom but only from the working of the living God in personal encounter.[75]

Mediated immediacy. Man's encounter with God brings him into a relationship of religious immediacy with the living God. This conception attests to the reality of a personal relationship with God and not to a relationship which is engendered inferentially. The nature of man's knowledge of God is not inferential but direct and intimate.[76]

> Yet, though we are more directly and intimately confronted with the presence of God than with any other presence, it does not follow that He is ever present to us apart from all other presences.[77]

The immediacy of God's presence is a "mediated immediacy."[78] God's presence is never perceived in isolation from human experience, but it always comes in and through familiar human experience. Nobody is able to see God with his corporeal eyes because God is not a corporeal being. His presence is always mediated to man through the context of familiar experience.[79] Theoretically there is no limit to the variety of media through which God's presence may be revealed. Historical events, the natural realm, and the Bible have been media through which God's presence has been made known.[80] Baillie observes that the chief medium of which the New Testament itself speaks and which governs all the rest is the Incarnation.[81]

Man's encounter with God does not occur in a vacuum but within the human situation. Man's religious experience with God is not an isolated matter that he may experience apart from the rest of his existence. The knowledge of God is given "only a being who is (a) self-conscious, (b) aware of other selves, and (c) aware of corporeal things."[82] The consciousness of God is never given unless it is in conjunction with the consciousness of things. God is not known through the world, but he is known with the world, and in knowing him with the world, he is known as its source and foundation. In this sense, Baillie believes, the world may become a sacramental universe which mediates to man the presence of God. The knowledge of God is not given in its isolated purity. God's revelation is given only in the context of the knowledge of finite realities. The finite realities can serve as media that lead man to a direct encounter with God.[83]

Man's knowledge of God is equally given "in, with and under" the knowledge of other persons. The life of humanity is understood by Baillie as being infinitely interwoven. Knowledge of God is indeed an intensely personal matter, but it can never be merely a private matter because man is never an isolated ego. The knowledge of God, then, is not given to those who are not involved in the service of their fellow men. In emphasizing the necessity of the Church, Baillie affirms that the knowledge of God comes to individuals only within the fellowship of faith. Thus in this sense, he believes, the Cyprianic formula, <u>extra ecclesiam nulla salus</u>, is true.[84]

The concept of mediated immediacy also points to the necessity of history in man's religious knowledge. God is mediated to man supremely through the Incarnation which is a historical event. Christ becomes the mediator that leads men to the gracious God.[85]

> The service of others, the fellowship with others, and the historical tradition in which I stand are all media that lead me to the Mediator, and the Mediator leads me to God. And all this mediation is part of God's gracious

purpose in refusing to unite me to Himself without at the same time uniting me to my fellow men--in making it impossible for me to obey either of the two great commandments without at the same time obeying the other.[86]

Personal knowledge. In man's knowledge of God, God meets man not as an object of knowledge but as a subject. "He is not something we find ourselves speaking about, but Some One we find speaking to us whom we then, in our turn, find ourselves speaking to."[87] God confronts us in such a direct and personal way that he is not spoken about but is addressed in the second person. There is no time when "third-person language" is fully appropriate to man's relationship with God since God is always the omnipresent Knower. He is always the subject and meets man in an "I-Thou" relationship, and this relationship can never be reduced to an "I-It" category.[88] Baillie regards the knowledge of persons as "the very type and pattern of what we mean by knowledge."[89] This knowledge is the most intimate and direct. The knowledge of God, just as the knowledge of the realities of man or the external world, is primary because it is apprehended in personal communion with God, who is the ultimate reality.[90]

Baillie is not willing to agree fully with Martin Buber's dislike of the term "experience of God." He contends that Buber's dislike of this phrase is mainly a verbal one. Buber is afraid to speak about the experience of God because this carries with it connotations of "making use of" or "turning to account." He believes that man only stands in personal relation to God and that he does not experience him. But Baillie believes that Buber's phrase, "experience of God," should be avoided and replaced by a concept that is more direct and personal.[91] Knowledge of God is founded on a personal relationship just as the knowledge of others is founded on the experience of their presence. This knowledge is not based on the discursive element of knowledge but on the perceptive or intuitive aspect of reason. No philosophical argument can prove the non-existence of a fellow man with whom one has had experience; nor can man be convinced that the existence of God is not real when he stands in personal relationship with him. "The most flawless proof of the existence of God is no substitute for it; and if we have that relationship the most convincing disproof is turned harmlessly aside."[92]

If God is the primary reality that confronts man, what is it that God reveals to man? Baillie teaches that the New Testament concept of revelation is the self-revelation of the divine personality. Revelation is always given within a personal relationship between subject and subject, and mind to mind.[93] God takes the initiative as a personal being in his revelation to make his presence known. What is revealed is God himself rather than truths about him. Personal fellowship with God is primary, and the knowledge of truths concerning him secondary.

> Certainly this is the kind of knowledge of which the New Testament speaks and which it so often designates as faith. "Ye have known God, or rather have been known by him." Characteristically and primarily faith is faith in God, confidence in him rather than the uttering of judgements concerning him.

. . . .

> We must say that our knowledge of the realities themselves--whether these be the external world or our fellow men or God--is primary, and our knowledge of truths concerning them secondary. The point, then, that I am most concerned to make is that, however difficult we may find it to ascribe certainty to these truths, we may nevertheless enjoy the certitude of having authentic acquaintance with the realities they fallibly seek to describe.[94]

Man is confronted not by an object of theoretical knowledge but with an absolute obligation. God's revelation is not given in propositional truths but through his self-communication. The truth, therefore, is not a truth about God's disclosure but the self-communication itself. What God gives is communion not information.[95] Baillie's position is succintly summed up in some quotations from William Temple: "What is offered to man's apprehension in any specific Revelation is not truth concerning God but the living God Himself."[96] Emphasizing again his disdain for a view which holds to revelation as propositional, Temple says:

> There is no such thing as revealed truth. There are truths of revelation, that is to say, propositions which express the result of correct thinking concerning revelation; but they are not themselves directly revealed.[97]

III. FAITH AS APPREHENSION AND RESPONSE

Faith as a primary mode of awareness. In Baillie's belief, faith is understood as a primary mode of awareness. It is by faith that a direct awareness of the reality of God is realized. This direct awareness is primary, and the propositional affirmations of the reality are secondary and derivative. Baillie has argued earlier for the direct realities of the external world, man himself, and his fellow man. God is also known directly. "Faith does not deduce from other realities that <u>are</u> present the existence of a God who is <u>not</u> present but absent; rather it is an awareness of the divine Presence itself."[98] Baillie has attempted to affirm the perceptional aspect of faith without denying the conceptional aspect. The "sense of the presence of God" or that "sense of duty" are perceptional modes which are beyond the ordinary sense of perception. Baillie calls man's response to these modes appreciation. Here appreciation is considered in the sense of an awareness of the claim made upon man from beyond himself and the "responsibility" that is demanded in that response. This is what Baillie calls "existential" thinking.[99]

The response to the divine claim made upon man is "obedient commitment." "Faith is thus at one and the same time a mode of apprehension and a mode of active response to that apprehension."[100] There can be, therefore, no apprehension without commitment and no commitment without apprehension. Faith includes both a cognitive and volitional element. Faith is a veridical apprehension of God as well as an obedient commitment to God; simultaneously it is an apprehension of his presence. Faith cannot be absolutely disjoined from assent to doctrinal truth, yet the distinction between faith and doctrine must be meticulously maintained. God himself is the revelation that comes in Christ, and no statements about him can ever bring man to the awareness of the God who is met directly.[101]

<u>Religious</u> <u>experience</u>. Faith, Baillie says, is the proper name for what man calls religious experience. The things of God are apprehended by faith. He does not believe that faith can be founded on religious experience. Baillie calls this view the "theology of experience" or the "Romanticist theory."[102] This theory, he states, seeks to substantiate religious convictions and beliefs by deducing them from religious experience which alone is supposed to constitute the substance of religion. Faith is said to rest on experience with God, and the love of God is trustworthy because it has been experienced as trustworthy. Since one's sins have been forgiven, he can believe in God's forgiveness. Since he has answered our prayer, he is known to be an "answerer of prayers." The "theory of religious experience" is dismissed by Baillie as untrue because he believes that faith is not based on religious experience, but that religious experience "if it is authentic, already <u>contains</u> faith."[103] Instead of calling faith a mode of experience, Baillie speaks of faith as a "mode of primary apprehension." Faith is the cognitive element in religious experience upon which the emotional and volitional elements are dependent.[104]

It is impossible to penetrate behind the reflective aspect of faith to an immediacy of content with God. Religious experience is essentially reflective in nature. All rational creatures have a religious consciousness. Religious belief is not consequent upon religious experience, but the religious experience and the belief are bound up in each other since religious experience is itself the experience of believing.[105]

> We can have no religious experience prior to and independently of religious faith, nor yet can we have any faith prior to and independently of the practical experience of religion--because religion is faith, and there is no religious experience of which faith is not a constituted part.[106]

It is impossible for a person to try to demonstrate the truth of his religious experience as one might demonstrate the validity of mathematical propositions. The criticisms by Immanuel Kant and David Hume of the rational arguments for the existence of God still hold validity and have never been fully answered; but even if they did not and these arguments were valid, it is still questionable whether that to which they finally arrive at in the process of the "proof" is worthy of worship. It may be only a "first cause," a "prime mover" or a "causal or theological factor" and not the God who comes to man in saving grace of which the New Testament bears witness. The "proofs" for the existence of God to demonstrate the evidence of God outside religious experience are doomed to failure. The so called "proofs" for the existence of God can have meaning only for those who are within the "circle of faith" who are willing to grant the basic presuppositions. Every proof is based on certain premises. Every proof seeks to derive conclusions from something that is given about something that is desired. If these premises are not accepted, then the argument is lost. The existence of God cannot be demonstrated to a person who is unwilling to believe. A casual reading of any book in religious philosophy reveals weaknesses within the proofs.[107] If a person has not had the necessary initial experience with God, he will not be led to that experience by argumentative "proofs." This personal experience with God is brought about by personal communion with God who takes the initiative in revelation. Man's response to revelation is a function of his total experience and not merely of the intellectual process.

Intuition. In the apprehension of the divine reality, Baillie believes that in man's religious insight the element of intuition is almost everything. "Intuitive insight will here always precede formal proof, and where there is as yet no such insight, formal proof is likely to be powerless to convince."[108] In his earlier works, The Roots of Religion in the

Human Soul and The Interpretation of Religion, Baillie sets forth an argument which is founded, not on an attempt to prove to unbelievers that God exists, but one which is based on an intuition of God which arises naturally from man's consciousness of duty.[109] In Our Knowledge of God, Baillie denies that man's religious knowledge is derivative in any sense.

> No proof of God's existence can help us to understand our faith in Him, or can in the last resort do anything but hinder such understanding, if it be true that it is not by a process of inference that our faith has actually been reached. And that I believe this to be true I have already sufficiently indicated. It is not as the result of an inference of any kind, whether explicit or implicit, whether laboriously excogitated or swiftly intuited, that the knowledge of God's reality comes to us. It comes rather through our direct personal encounter with Him in the Person of Jesus Christ His Son our Lord.[110]

In his Gifford Lectures, Baillie places a strong emphasis on the intuited element within man. Here he attempts to draw together both perspectives, the intuitive and the non-inferential. "All in all, therefore, the seat of human wisdom will always remain with our intuited rather than with our inferred knowledge of our human situation."[111] He has not stated with clearness what he means by intuition, however, he has disassociated himself from the view that intuition is an apprehension of a truth or a proposition.[112] This emphasis on the intuited element has been variously called by Baillie as "non-sensuous perception," "apprehending an aspect of reality," and "the sense of the presence of God."[113] Baillie's concept of knowledge places the emphasis on direct insight, or immediate awareness of truth which carries with it greater certainty than inferential knowledge.

Douglas Clyde Macintosh has argued that Baillie's intuitive view of epistemology is both dogmatic and agnostic. He avers that Baillie's view of knowing not only the reality of God but his personality, goodness, infinity, eternity, omniscience, and omnipotence by direct acquaintance and not by inference brings him under the suspicion of being "unduly dogmatic."[114] This is the age old problem of what kinds of principles are intuitive. There are various schools of thought on this problem. It may be granted that an intuition may be a dream or a phantasm instead of a veridical perception, but who is to determine when a fundamental or genuine intuition has taken place? If an intuition is considered by itself, it is impossible to ascertain its validity or falsity. Even mathematical truths ultimately rest on axioms which cannot be proved but are considered to be self-evident. So intuitive truth cannot be used as the testing ground to determine the validity of truth but only as the axiomatic arena from which deduction may legitimately originate. Baillie's claim to direct knowledge of God may be looked upon by some as being dogmatic, but this same accusation can be directed against any truth which is claimed to be intuited.

By means of argumentation, one deduces a desired reality from one already known. This previously known reality may have been deduced from another reality which was prior to one's knowledge of the other. The only way that this fallacy of an infinite regress can be avoided, Baillie believes, is by establishing one's belief on some reality which is known in a direct manner and not by deduction. This places the emphasis on immediacy rather than the discursive element in knowledge. Baillie illustrates his position by drawing two analogies from Kierkegaard. This immediate reality is like the brick laid directly on the ground which becomes the foundation upon which the rest are placed, and like the knot that is needed in the thread in order to sew. There is the need, then, for a reality which confronts man directly and is the ground of knowledge which itself is not deduced from something else.[115] This prime reality is the living God himself. "The witness of all true religion is that there is no reality which more directly confronts us than the reality of God."[116]

Practical reason. Indicating a Kantian influence, Baillie places the emphasis on the primacy of practical reason. Ultimate reality is conceived not as an object of speculation or theoretical knowledge but as an absolute obligation. Baillie differs with Kant in his interpretation of the relation of faith to guidance. Kant believed that the obligation was presented as a "self-evidencing law" detached from God and that the knowledge of God is derived by inference from the obligation. Baillie, on the other hand, argues that the absolute obligation can only be revealed by the Absolute and that the source of the obligation is God himself who is directly revealed. God challenges us by being what in essence he is and not by exhortation of what he is not. In his revelation God is personally disclosed,[117] and he is known as the primary reality.[118]

The *legitimacy* of *personal* encounter. Baillie's position is certainly well founded. It has not only the support of the biblical record[119] but almost all of contemporary theological thought. In his book, The Idea of Revelation in Recent Thought, Baillie gives quotation after quotation from theologians such as William Temple, A. G. Hebert, Emil Brunner, Karl Barth, A. E. Taylor, Frederick R. Tennant and many others to show their stress on the personal revelation of God himself to man rather than propositional truths about him.[120]

Baillie's position is well expressed in the following statement:

> Revelation essentially consists not in the communication of truths about God but in the self-revelation of the divine Personality, the truths about Him being abstracted by ourselves from the concrete reality with which we thus become acquainted, and our knowledge of his existence being given in and with the revelation rather than guessed at in advance of it.[121]

Baillie's view of knowledge by personal encounter seems justified on several grounds. If it is God who encounters man as the divine subject, then the fallacies of subjectivism and objectivism are avoided. Subjectivism is avoided because the initiative in the act of revelation comes not from within man himself, but outside of man as he is confronted by the Absolute. Man is not able by his own efforts to arrive at a knowledge of God, but he is encountered by the living Word who makes his presence known to him. Objectivism seeks to reduce God to a thing, an "it," instead of a "Thou" who confronts man. Objectivism is the attempt to absolutize the word of God in terms of doctrines or a book. Since all objective knowledge is impersonal and can be controlled by man, God can never be understood as an object waiting to be known. He is the divine subject. He makes himself known and is not controlled. Communion with God is always personal and cannot be equated with knowledge of data or facts. Baillie's position of the knowledge of God as a personal being who makes his presence known to man in a vital personal encounter eludes, in the writer's opinion, the weaknesses of subjectivism and objectivism.

Trust and assent. The knowledge of persons is considered by Baillie to be the "very type and pattern of what we mean by knowledge."[122] The knowledge of persons is the most intimate and direct. The term "know" is used primarily in reference to persons and not things. The knowledge of persons is the kind of knowledge of which the New Testament speaks and is the designation that is used to describe the Christian's faith.[123] The knowledge of God is personal and therefore is the most intimate and direct way man can commune with God. Today, almost all theologians are willing to agree that God reveals himself personally. The problem, however, usually centers around the question whether there can be knowledge about God in this revelation. A problem is raised in consideration of the relationship of trust to assent.

Throughout his theology Baillie has contended that the Christian faith is essentially trust. Trust is man's complete reliance on God and his commitment fully to God's guardianship.[124] The element of commitment takes precedence over assent to propositional truths about God. Baillie states that he has always been careful to add "that there are certain intellectual implicates latently contained in such trust."[125] Trust in God is based on grounds for this trust; yet it is difficult to express in verbal form what these grounds are.

> When I trust somebody, or have <u>fiducia</u> in him, I am manifestly at the same time believing certain things about him to be true, yet I may find it very difficult to say exactly what these things are--I may even flounder helplessly in the attempt to assign the reasons for my trust.[126]

In an earlier work, Baillie has stated that the primary meaning of faith to Jesus was reliance or trust and not credence. Trust is man's willingness to cast himself without fear upon the love of God. However, in this work there is also the emphasis that even in man's reliance on God an element of credence is "explicitly or implicitly contained." Man cannot put his trust in a God that he does not believe to exist or who he believes is not worthy of the confidence placed in him. Here again Baillie places the emphasis on the point that credence grows out of the trust rather than being its sole source.[127] He expresses this same truth in <u>Our Knowledge of God</u> when he speaks of the truths about God being abstracted from the reality of his presence rather than being conjectured about before the actual experience has taken place.[128] In man's encounter with God he commits himself in trust to God, and out of this commitment grows the certainty of God's reality and his worthiness to be trusted. This certainty is not reached by committing one's self to the truthfulness of certain propositions before this experience has transpired. Trust in God does not come about by "purely intellectual paths of discovery." Faith is not an assent to propositions but trust in the personal God.[129]

> Christian faith does not mean believing a number of things, few or many: it means a single indivisible disposition of mind and heart. It does not mean accepting a creed: it means trusting in God.[130]

Traditional orthodoxy has contended that propositional revelation is the only genuine medium that can lead a man to a confrontation with the living Word.[131] This, however, is the very thing that Baillie is denying. Doctrine is an outgrowth of the encounter not a prerequisite of faith. The knowledge of God is not propositional or inferential but is personal and immediate. Any knowledge about God is received in and with the event of revelation and not formulated and affirmed prior to the encounter.

πιστεύω ὅτι or πιστεύω εἰς and ἐν. Commitment takes precedence over assent. Although one can find some use of the words "believe that" (πιστεύω ὅτι) in the Scriptures, the usual formulation is "believe in" (πιστεύω εἰς or ἐν). The latter expresses personal trust and reliance as being distinct from mere belief. Baillie observes that even in the Apostles' and Nicene Creeds the confession is not "belief that" certain things are true about God and Christ and the Holy Spirit, but rather "belief in."[132] "It is πιστεύω εἰς, not ὅτι: credo in, not credo with an accusative and infinitive. The element of commitment here clearly takes precedence over the element of assent."[133] A correspondence is needed between the understanding of the revelation as it is given and the understanding of the reception of it by faith. Faith is primarily trust instead of assent since God's revelation is personal rather than propositional. The Christian faith is basically a reliance upon God's revelation in Christ. In this trust there is presupposed a necessary acquaintance with its object and latently an assent to certain affirmations that can be made about the object.[134] Here Baillie quotes 2 Timothy 1:12 to establish his argument: "I know whom I have believed." But his emphasis is that in the encounter the trust always precedes assent. He also observes that it is in the Athanasian Creed that one finds the exception to the usual form of "belief in." Athanasius lists a long number of theological propositions which he states that a man has to believe if he is to be saved.[135] This is the very thing that Baillie objects to in propositional revelation.

One of the central themes of H. D. Lewis' book, Our Experience of God, is his insistence that man cannot have an encounter with God independently of some knowledge "about" him. "I do not know what it would mean at all to encounter God independently of what I believe His character and activity to be or what He requires of me in some situation."[136] He declares that man cannot just cry "encounter," but that he must realize that there are some definite things that are true about God. Lewis' basic presupposition is that God is a personal being addressing himself to individuals and present to them. Religious experience, he declares, involves this from the beginning because the reality encountered in religion presents itself as personal although the recognition of this fact may not always be clear.[137] He argues further:

> In any case, all the expedients to which I have briefly referred have to encounter, in addition to the difficulty they involve in general as theories of knowledge, the special difficulty of showing how significant assertions can be made at all about a mystery which is by its very nature, and the mode of our acknowledging it, bound to

be incomprehensible.138

Although it is not clear what truths Lewis believes have been revealed, it is very clear what he believes has not been revealed: "It is wrong also, in my opinion, to suppose that what we have in religious experience is some direct assurance of the truth of some general notion like theological doctrines."139 He believes that when man encounters God this experience is mediated through forms of one's own day. Lewis goes on to insist that this experience cannot be articulated to others in any way other than by the use of religious symbols and by a life that pulsates within by this vital experience and reflects outwardly what has happened within. He is very forceful in his insistence that no type of dogma can be established which man must believe. This abuse of dogma he calls idolatry.140 In many ways there is a similarity between Lewis' thought and Baillie's. They both emphasize encounter and intuition and reject propositional revelation. Lewis, in many ways, speaks in a similar vein about the way one arrives at a knowledge about God. He desires to expound how one has a knowledge about God in this encounter, but his answer is not as clear as the one established by Baillie. Yet, Baillie is certainly an "encounter" theologian against whom Lewis' argument would seem to be directed. However, the parallel between much of their thought is striking.

Baillie's view certainly commends itself above the traditional view he is rejecting. Faith is basically trust and not simply belief. All trust includes some element of belief, but this knowledge is given in and with the personal encounter not apart from it. Theology aids in clarifying one's faith, and the theological description is always secondary to the vital experience itself and can never be equated with the reality it seeks to describe. Faith is always primary, and belief is secondary. Traditional orthodoxy seeks to maintain that revelation cannot be known apart from a verbal form. If the verbal form is said to be expressed only within the Scriptures today, even then the problem is still not resolved. It is granted that God speaks through the medium of the written word today, but the willingness of traditional orthodoxy to affirm a general revelation of God is tantamount to acknowledging that the written word is not the only medium through which he speaks. It is also not true to human experience to say that there can be no experience of another without the passing of a word. Conversation is an intimate means of communion, but it is not the only means, nor is it the first. Men had communion with one another before speech was developed. Even today with speech, communion can be established by a nod, a gesture, a glance, a touch, a facial motion or a body motion. Communion can be established in a vital way without a verbal word passing. There can be an intercourse of minds through a non-verbal articulation. This is seen in the love of a mother for her baby or in the love between a husband and his wife. Since God is a spiritual being and closer to man than breath itself, communion with him can be personal and intimate without the necessity of verbal encounter. Since a savage, a child or even those who are mute and inarticulate can experience the reality of God's presence, revelation can never be reduced to a verbal form.

God's revelation is not static truth that waits to be discovered but personal truth that is always seeking to make itself known. Even the statement presented in propositional form, "God is love," (I John 4:8) is not the same type of truth as the static, mathematical truth that two times two equals four. This mathematical truth can be demonstrated in a scientific and logical way, but no one can demonstrate, in a scientific way, that "God is love." This truth can be read by many, but the reality of God as love will not be realized until God has been experienced as love. One cannot arrive at the knowledge of the nature of God by inference but only by personal revelation. Jesus Christ is the objectification in time of God's eternal love. In him is seen the fullness of God's love. (John 3:16, I John 4:7-10) Apart from the personal revelation of God in Christ, the terms, "God's love" and "Jesus is Lord," have no meaning. The meaning is given in and with the event itself. They are not static propositions that can be arrived at by scientific methods, but truth which is actualized in a personal sense. The same is true of the confession of the primitive Christian community, "Jesus is Lord." Is this a proposition that one assents to or is "Jesus Lord" only to those who have experienced him as Lord? Jesus Christ is certainly Lord eternally, but he becomes Lord to a man only when that individual commits his life in trust to him having been led by the spirit of God to the one who is the truth.

Hic et nunc. In his view of revelation as *hic et nunc*, "here and now," Baillie has reaffirmed his belief that the revelation of God comes in conjunction of immediacy with mediacy. God reveals himself to man in the past, but God's revelation to those in the past was given to them while it was still present for them. No one could find the presence of God now in the apostolic interpretation of the Gospel or the prophetic interpretation of God's dealing with Israel if God had not been contemporary with them. Contemporary man, Baillie asserts, may be aware that God was evident in these past events because he is presently revealing himself to man. The *Testimonium internum Spiritus Sancti* gives credence to the *hic et nunc* of God's activity with man. By looking with those in the past at the revelatory events, those in the present become contemporaneous with them. This becomes for modern man the "existential moment."[141]

God has revealed himself in the fellowship of his Church. Within the corporate community of <u>Koinonia</u> God's revelation is given. God's revelation reaches individual man as it is mediated through the Church. In the fellowship of the Church God's revelation is given to the individual man in the present moment.[142]

<u>Ways</u> <u>of</u> <u>believing</u>. In referring to the universality of man's knowledge of God, Baillie has set forth a curious formula to state ways of believing in God. He contends that although some may deny God with the "top of their minds," they in some sense believe in him in the "bottom of their hearts." All belief, he is convinced, must be conscious but not necessarily conscious of itself. In this respect, Baillie has been influenced by Cook Wilson who presented a paper to the Oxford Society in 1897 entitled "Rational Grounds of Belief in God."[143] Following this viewpoint, Baillie states that the intellectual denial of God's existence need not completely destroy one's spiritual life.

> Just as the intellectual affirmation of God's existence is not of itself sufficient to initiate the soul's communion with God, so the corresponding denial is not of itself sufficient to destroy that communion. After all, the central thing in religion is not our hold on God but God's hold on us; not our choosing Him but His choosing us; not that we should know Him but that we should be known of Him.[144]

A distinction is made by Baillie between different kinds of knowledge. There is a knowledge of God which goes deeper than one's denial of the reality of God's existence. Although man may deny God intellectually, there is an unconscious faith deep within him which, when brought to clear faith, is discovered to be not a <u>de</u> <u>novo</u> discovery of God, but a disclosure that all the time he has been believing in God.[145]

More serious in its distinction of the spiritual life of man than the intellectual denial of God's existence is the practical denial. Baillie argues that the man who claims he believes in the existence of God, but lives as if God does not exist, comes closer to denying God's existence than one who denies him intellectually. His life demonstrates to others that he does not really believe what he thinks he believes.[146]

Although man may know God in the bottom of his heart while denying him with the top of his mind, Baillie affirms that he cannot know God well. This denial threatens the foundation of the spiritual life even if it does not utterly destroy it. Unconscious faith is certainly inadequate for proper Christian growth.[147] The believer is able to see in the familiar experiences of life a meaning that the unbeliever can never detect. "It is impossible that the spiritual life should ever flourish save in the generous atmosphere of an unabridged Christian profession and practice."[148] But a few pages later Baillie states that the man who doubts or denies God with the top of his mind, by the grace of God, may possess the _forma fidei essentialis_.[149] Thus, "unself-conscious" faith may be a _fides salvifica_. He believes that there must be allowed the possibility of a "justification of the doubter" as well as the "justification of the sinner." Yet, he is aware that there can be no justification for one who denies God if faith is understood as being necessarily conscious of itself in order to be genuine.[150]

Baillie is convinced, then, that some men may have faith without knowing it; but he is quick to state that, in speaking of unconscious faith, one is not to use this as an excuse for his own unbelief, but he is to apply it in charity toward his neighbor. Quoting John Ker, he concurs that "'there is such a thing as unconscious faith, but those who plead it in their own behalf do not possess it. With them it is conscious unbelief.'"[151]

As enticing as Baillie's view of unconscious faith may appear, there are some features of this theory that conflict with other aspects of his theology. Baillie's chief thesis in all of his writings has been that man knows God by being personally confronted by him. If man has been confronted by the holy presence of God, he may not grasp all that is involved in this encounter, but surely he must be conscious of this relationship for it to be meaningful to him. If man's faith is still on the unconscious level, can one claim that in reality this faith has risen to a genuine level of awareness? It seems that this cannot be allowed. There is within everyone the striving of God's spirit to motivate him to an awareness of the living God; but until this experience arises to a conscious level, man's relationship to God cannot be spoken of as a "faith relationship." Were man able unconsciously to have faith in God, then his freedom would seriously be threatened after he consciously has disavowed any belief in God.

In another article, Baillie has clearly stated that the revelation of God's presence comes not "in dim, instinctive semicerebral psychosis but in the fullest light of human intelligence."[152] If revelation is not given to our subconscious mind, can it then be contained in our unconscious mind? According to Baillie, faith is a direct awareness of the reality of God which issues in a response by man. Man is made aware of the claim that is made upon him, and his response to the divine claim is "obedient commitment."[153] He states that there can be no apprehension without commitment and no commitment without apprehension. Faith includes both a cognitive and a volitional element.[154] In his Gifford Lectures Baillie appears to have forsaken the view of unconscious faith in the selection just mentioned. But in his discussion on whether faith is ever completely lost, he still seems to be advocating a position not dissimilar to the one set forth in Our Knowledge of God.[155] Has not Baillie, however, touched the heart of the problem dealing with unconscious faith when he spoke about commitment? It is evident there can be no genuine faith without commitment, and commitment may only be realized on a conscious level. Man is confronted by God on the conscious level and responds or rejects the summons to commitment in a selfconscious awareness of the presence of God.

Nature and grace. Baillie is unwilling to allow a dichotomy between the state of nature and the state of grace. He believes that there is no point at which an absolute line can be determined below which God's grace does not extend. He advocates a continuity between the natural and the spiritual life. That which is deepest in nature leads to grace and glory.[156]

Various theologians are considered by Baillie on this problem, but they are viewed as unsatisfactory if they do not subscribe to the principle of continuity. Baillie's view of revelation, including general revelation, is understood in its true perspective only when all revelation is realized to be special in the sense that it is God's self-disclosure. This view of revelation allows him to speak, therefore, of a "general grace." If God's grace is revealed in a universal or general sense to man, then, it is also saving grace. Every soul that responds to the truth of God, even when in good faith he is in error or denies God's existence, will, in reality, not be beyond the grace of God. God's revelation wherever it occurs brings with it salvation.[157]

> Salvation means fellowship with God. The state of being saved is the state of being in fellowship with Him. To believe that some men are wholly out of such fellowship is the same as to believe that they are totally corrupt; for good in the creature can result only from fellowship with the Creator, who is the alone Source of all the good there is. But I have already argued that a creature from which the image of God was thus wholly effaced would not any longer be a man at all.[158]

Baillie does not appreciate the point of difference that is made by those that seek to establish a dichotomy between general and special revelation. He argues that this dichotomy issues in a distinction being made between sustaining grace and saving grace. He believes that nothing is gained in admitting a continuity between nature and grace if the continuity that exists between the grace that sustains and the grace that saves is denied. There is no gracious element about a sustaining grace which does not save.[159] Baillie believes that the answer to this problem is realized in the understanding of the nature of the "Eternal Spirit" and "Presence" of God. Wherever in the world there has been any real knowledge of and communion with the "Divine Father," it has been the result of the impact of the same Spirit and Presence of God that was finally made manifest in Jesus of Nazareth. The same *Logos* was dealing with men wherever a revelation of God was disclosed whether it was to Moses, David, Jeremiah or even Socrates, Plato or Zeno.[160] The knowledge of God known by the men of the Old Testament and other ancient times was mediated through the eternal Son of God, though he had not yet been made flesh. The mediation of his revelation was through One whose name was not rightly known until later.[161]

The concept of continuity as held by Baillie is rendered more understandable when it is realized that all revelation, in his thought, is special and must at the same time be gracious. This, he believes, is realizable when the Christian acknowledges the reality not only of the "eternal Son of God" but the reality of an "eternal atonement."

In a quotation from his late brother, D. M. Baillie, John Baillie sets forth a summary account of his position:

> To reduce the importance of the historical event would be contrary to every instinct of the Christian faith; and yet it seems impossible to say that the divine sin-bearing was confined to that moment of time, or is anything less than eternal . . . As God was incarnate in Jesus, so we may say that the divine Atonement was incarnate in the passion of Jesus. And if we then go on to speak of an eternal Atonement in the very life and being of God, it is not by way of reducing the significance of the historical moment of the Incarnation, but by way of realizing the relation of the living God to every historical moment. God's reconciling work cannot be confined to any one moment of history. We cannot say that God was unforgiving until Christ came and died on Calvary; nor can we forget that God's work of reconciliation still goes on in every age in the lives of sinful men, whose sins He still bears.[162]

Salvation, then, Baillie believes, is to be found only in Jesus Christ. Salvation is found only in the "way of Christ." When Baillie allows for salvation to be acknowledged in any revelation of God's presence, he is careful to assert that this saving power is not apart from Christ. "The Eternal Christ who was made <u>flesh</u> in Jesus of Nazareth, and the Eternal Atonement which was made event on Calvary, were and are the source of every 'saving process.'"163

Baillie's position seems well founded when he advocates a correlation between revelation and redemption. If God has made his presence manifest, can the redemptive aspect be separated from the revelatory? God's presence has been disclosed through historical events and men have responded. Is it logical to maintain that Moses, Isaiah and others were excluded from his gracious activity? It seems closer to the truth to acknowledge an interaction between God's divine revelation and his redemptive activity. Before the <u>Logos</u> was made flesh, he moved within the hearts of men. The manifestation of God's grace revealed in Jesus of Nazareth is the actualization within time of the eternal grace of God. The love of God revealed in Jesus was the projection in history of the eternal love of God. The grace and love of God revealed in Jesus of Nazareth is the revelation of the eternal nature of the love and grace of God who has always been seeking to make his presence known and acknowledged by men. Wherever the eternal Son has made his presence known and men have responded in trust, then this self-same revelation is redemptive.164

No statement about the relationship between the state of nature and the state of grace can be fully adequate. The apparent incompatibility between these two states need not be absolute. There will remain an element of tension between continuity and discontinuity, but the truth involved in both aspects may be expressed either way as Edgar Primrose Dickie has declared:

> (1) There is continuity, but nevertheless something that is absolutely new comes into being; or (2) There is discontinuity, yet the good that was in the old is not annihilated but fulfilled.165

<u>Conversion</u> <u>and</u> <u>Baptism</u>. A final word needs to be mentioned before concluding this section on faith and grace. Baillie has criticized sharply the Christian groups which call for a crisis experience of conversion. "I should therefore very much deprecate any teaching which makes everything hinge upon a single conversional readjustment, so as to demand or encourage it in every case."166 He argues that this sort of emphasis tends to lead to mental distress and places too much reliance upon a single point in a person's life and may cause him to consider further growth or reformation unnecessary. What he considers to be significant is not that someone has had a particular sort of an experience, but rather that

his experiences should be Christian whatever they are. The important thing is not a gradual adjustment or a sudden readjustment, but that in the end men should have the "authentic and full Christian outlook."[167]

In attempting to affirm the legitimacy of infant baptism, Baillie has noted that this act marks for the infant the real beginning of the Christian life within the Christian community. The infant is to "grow up in the faith" until he reaches the point of sealing the commitment which was made for him by his own deliberate decision.[168] Baillie suggests that Baptists believe children are hopelessly lost until they reach the state of maturity and make their own commitment.[169] Baptist groups today certainly have not expounded this view. A child's fate, according to Baptist theology, has always been left in the gracious hands of a loving God. A child is not held responsible until he arrives at an age when he possesses a knowledge of good and evil. As a child, he is in God's gracious favor by having been created in his image and not because of a sacramental rite performed by the Church. When a person reaches the age of accountability, he or she must make his or her own commitment for or against God. No one else can do this for him. One's relationship with God is never on a second-hand basis, but must always be experiential. Baillie speaks of the necessity of a commitment, but then refers to a commitment made "for" another.[170] How can this be in experimental religion? One's commitment to God must be conscious, necessarily free, and voluntary. An inner experience with God cannot be compelled nor can a commitment be made for someone else. H. Wheeler Robinson has stated the Baptist position well on the reason for "believers'" baptism which is administered on a profession of personal faith in Christ:

> The common element in all these interpretations of baptism is the necessary _passivity_ of the infant baptized. Whether baptism be called dedication, or covenanting by parents, or the sealing of a divine covenant, or an actual regeneration, it is throughout something done to, nothing done by, the baptized. So far as he is concerned, all of them are non-moral acts, though the act of the parents or sponsors is properly moral. The Baptist position is not simply a new phase of this succession of interpretations; it stands outside of them all as <u>the only baptism which is strictly and primarily an ethical act on the part of the baptized.</u>[171]

George R. Beasley-Murray has presented another contemporary Baptist theologian's view on believers' baptism.

Against every tendency of New Testament theologians to minimize the Pauline doctrine of faith it must be insisted that in his teaching faith in God manifested in Christ is _prior_ to baptism, and faith receives the gift of God _in_ baptism, and faith in God is the constitutive principle of the Christian life _after_ baptism. There is not a line in Paul's writings that justifies a reversal of this emphasis in the relationship between the two.[172]

Baptists have historically called for a regenerate church membership. Baptism is administered only to "believers." E. Y. Mullins stated in _The Axioms of Religion_ that "the ecclesiastical significance of Baptists is a regenerated church-membership."[173] One of the early Baptist Confessions of Faith, dated August 10, 1656, affirmed this belief:

"That in admitting of members into the church of Christ, it is the duty of the church, and ministers whom it concerns, in faithfulness to God, that they be careful they receive none but such as do make forth evident demonstration of the new birth, and the work of faith with power."[174]

Recently Baptist theologians themselves have acknowledged that many Baptist churches have not always measured up in practice to their ideal of believers' baptism. This has been particularly true where the age at baptism has gradually been lowered to accommodate younger and younger children. This practice has come under sharp attack by many Baptist theologians.[175]

Few Baptist theologians would be willing to say that conversion is limited to a sudden event that is completed and finalized in a few moments.[176] Baillie is certainly correct when he states that is a life long process. Nevertheless, has he not come close to the Baptist position when he quotes Alex Vidler in apparent agreement? "There must be, in one way or another this initial conversion, this decisive self-commitment."[177] And again when he quotes from another, J. Fraster McLuskey, who declares that decisions may occur in different ways "but however they are made, they must be made at least once."[178] This is the very fact that Baptists are advocating, self-conscious commitment. Redemption is a life long process, but it has its initial beginning in a faith commitment to the living Lord. As Robinson has so aptly stated it: "The true emphasis is that of the New Testament—on personal faith as the human condition of divine activity, which is the truth supremely expressed in believers' baptism."[179]

Karl Barth entered the theological world by presenting a challenge whose fervor is still sweltering today. He concluded his theological writings with the same kind of challenge with which he began and which has, for the most part, been almost completely ignored. His words present the "summons to contest" when he declares that "the practice of infant baptism is profoundly irregular."

> To all concerned: to theologians, for unfortunately even theology has not yet realized by a long way that infant baptism is an ancient ecclesiastical error; to Christian congregations and their pastors; to Church leaders, presbyterial, synodal or episcopal; to all individual Christians, however simple, let it be said that they should see to it whether they can and will continue to bear responsibility for what has become the dominant baptismal practice, whether they might not and must not dare to face up to the wound from which the Church suffers at this genuinely vital point with its many-sided implications, whether they could not and should not undertake measures for its healing which do not bear the character of compromise and which ought not, therefore, to be the last to call for consideration.[180]

Barth's earlier tract, <u>The Teaching of the Church Regarding Baptism</u>, delivered on May 7, 1943 at Gwatt, Switzerland, was his first attempt to demonstrate on biblical, theological and practical basis that a baptized person cannot be merely passive, but he must be an active participant if the act of baptism is to be meaningful to him. He asserted that baptism should be a free, responsible, cognitive act on the part of a confessing Christian and not a causative action.[181] In the preface to the final volume of his <u>Church Dogmatics</u>, Barth acknowledges the reaction he anticipates to his final words.

> I foresee that this book, which by human judgment will be my last major publication, will leave me in the theological and ecclesiastical isolation which has been my lot for almost fifty years. I am thus about to make a poor exit with it. So be it! The day will come when justice will be done to me in this matter too.[182]

Barth was aware of the emotional nature of the gauntlet he had cast down before the Church. He knew how difficult it would be to break through church tradition and theological systems. Baillie, in his concept of religious knowledge, failed to apply his understanding of man's knowledge of God in a meaningful way to the act of baptism itself. Here his basic presupposition was not carried through to make the act of baptism a cognitive, personal one for the individual being baptized. Barth's challenge still affords the church the occasion for some introspection regarding the teaching and practice of baptism.[183]

CHAPTER IV

RELIGIOUS KNOWLEDGE AND THE LANGUAGE OF FAITH

Without a doubt one of the most pressing contemporary problems relevant to the question of revelation is the relationship of language to religious knowledge. The impact of logical positivism and linguistic philosophy has placed this problem in the foreground of much of the present day dialogue between philosophy and theology. In the center of this discussion of the language of religion should be the role of the Bible. In this chapter an examination will be made of the following aspects of religious knowledge and the language of faith: the role of the Bible in the language of faith; the role of language in religious knowledge; and the method used for verification of religious knowledge.

I. THE ROLE OF THE BIBLE IN RELIGIOUS KNOWLEDGE

All Christians believe that the Bible has a unique role in the Church and the Christian way of life. The resurgence of biblical theology is a strong witness to this fact. Baillie, like most religious thinkers, has been impressed by the impact of the movement and has been influenced by it, but he has, nevertheless, sought to maintain the truth which he has seen in many perspectives. As an eclectic thinker, Baillie has drawn and sifted in his mind what he considers to be the best thought in various traditions. Although he maintains that there is a necessary distinction between Scripture and revelation, he believes that there is a positive relation of Scripture to revelation.[1] The relationship of the Scriptures to revelation is correctly discerned when the nature and purpose of the Bible is comprehended.

<u>Nature and purpose of the Scriptures</u>. The central purpose of the Bible is to declare <u>Heilsgeschichte,</u> the redemptive activity of God in history. The uniqueness of the Scriptures as revelatory is realized in the role it bears as the medium which contains the record of God's redemptive activity.[2] "The Bible is the written witness to that intercourse of mind and event which is the essence of revelation."[3] The Bible relates the divine activity of God with mankind as he revealed himself through historical events, climaxing his revelation in Jesus Christ. Baillie has rejected the view of the nature of the Bible as a manual of doctrinal information. He believes that God reveals himself not in the forms of communication but of communion.[4] "God does not communicate with us," Baillie states, "He does something far better--He communes with us.

Not the communication of propositions but the communion of spirits is the last word about divine revelation."5 Since God's revelation is always personal, the purpose of the Scriptures is to bear witness to the personal one who is seeking to make himself known to the minds and hearts of all men. The nature of the revelation of which the Scriptures bear witness was given in personal, historical events, therefore, the purpose of the Scriptures is to bear witness to the <u>Heilsgeschichte,</u> the redemptive activity of God. The Scriptures serve as a medium to mediate the immediacy of the living God. 6

Baillie is insistent that the burden of the <u>Kerygma</u> of the early disciples which later was included in the Scriptures was motivated by something that God was doing in a decisive way in history. God's mighty activity within history was the good news. It is at this point that Baillie believes that the Christian <u>Kerygma</u> is different from all other religions. Christianity calls men not to assent to a system of propositions but to place their trust in the redemptive activity of God. The nature of the Bible can, therefore, never be described as "propositional revelation."7 The nature of the Bible is always involved in its basic purpose which is to bear witness to the redemptive activity of God.

> And this is the essential respect in which the Christian kerygma differs from that of all other religions. It calls men, not to give assent to a system of abstract notions, but to put their trust in something that happened, laying their minds open to the decisive significance of it, and allowing it to be decisive for them in their own personal and community life. Christianity had its origin not in something men did or in something they thought or believed, but in something that happened to them. And to this day what makes a man a Christian is not anything he does, nor, in the last resort, is it anything he thinks or believes, but something that happens to him. 8

<u>Inspiration of Scripture.</u> In Baillie's opinion, the concept of inspiration is the necessary counterpart of the concept of revelation.9 Every concept of revelation entails a concept of inspiration. Just as he has insisted that revelation is personal, he also affirms his belief that God's inspiration is personal. A book or an utterance is not inspired, but the one who wrote the book or articulated the utterance is inspired.

> It is not in words and books that God reveals Himself, but in men; not in tables of stone but in the tables of

the human heart. God is in words and books only because He is in the men behind the words and books.[10]

Throughout his writings, his emphasis has been on the personal character of both revelation and inspiration. "God is in books only because He was in the men behind the books. An inspired book means properly a book written by an inspired man."[11]

Revelation involves not only a disclosure by God in history but is not completed until there is an intercourse of event and interpretation. The revelatory activity of God's nature is witnessed not only in his mighty acts but in the illumination of the minds of the prophetic and apostolic believers. God not only revealed himself in redemptive activity but inspired men so they would be able to grasp the significance of the revelation. After the illumination of man by God, the witness came. The Scriptures are the written witness to the intercourse of event and interpretation. Baillie notes that the witness to the intercourse of events and illumination is a human activity and, therefore, is not infallible. But he believes that God who had performed his mighty acts and illumined men's minds would not leave the prophetic and apostolic testimony unaided. Just as God's spirit had led men into salvation, he must also have guided their endeavors to communicate the gospel. This, Baillie states, is the meaning of the inspiration of the Scriptures.[12]

The point which has continued to provoke discussion among Christians has been over the matter of "plenary" inspiration. This concept of inspiration would make the control of God's spirit so complete that human fallibility would be superseded. Baillie observes that this has been the prevailing view of the Roman Catholic Church and traditional Protestant orthodoxy. The Roman Church has also claimed that in the Pope an inerrant interpreter of Scripture has been provided for each age.[13]

Although Baillie rejects any notion of a dictation theory of inspiration and also acknowledges the fallibility of the human aspect of the written witness, he subscribes to a belief of verbal inspiration if it is not regarded as plenary.[14] He holds to a verbal and conceptual view of inspiration. He does not hesitate to affirm that inspiration extends not only to the thoughts of the writers but to the very words they used to express their thoughts. Nevertheless, neither thought inspiration nor verbal inspiration is understood as plenary by him. He states that it is impossible to separate the thoughts of Paul, Isaiah and the other writers from their language.[15]

As it is evident from the above discussion, Baillie does not believe that words and ideas can be separated. But traditional orthodoxy can take little comfort in using Baillie's position to support its own view of verbal inspiration. In rejecting the "plenary" aspect of inspiration, Baillie has made allowance for the fallible aspects of the written witness to be recognized, and he will, in no sense, allow that every word of the Scripture is equally inspired.[16] In discussing the relationship of words and ideas in inspiration, Dewey M. Beegle has laid down a principle which is expressive of Baillie's view: "A true concept necessitates correct key words, but there may well be some inaccurate details that are incidental to the argument or presentation of the chief idea."[17]

Baillie's view of "verbal inspiration" certainly produces problems which he could not easily resolve. Since he himself had sought to separate the pre-Copernican and even the pre-Ptolemaic cosmography of the Scriptures from the essential revelation, he was surely aware that this disentanglement made his view of verbal and conceptual inspiration difficult to support. Having rejected plenary inspiration, Baillie does not need to justify how every word and idea is inspired, but he does have to justify how he can believe certain words and thoughts are inspired verbally without his view eventually ending in a dictation concept of inspiration. If the word and thoughts are both from God, then in what sense is the message adapted to the world view and intelligence of the one through whom the message comes? Why does Baillie feel the necessity of speaking of verbal inspiration at all? He has indicated that the purpose of Scripture is to bear witness to the revelation instead of being identified with the whole of revelation.[18] So, his view of verbal inspiration is not necessary to his argument and, in fact, makes it difficult to establish. If the Scriptures are the witness to the revelation, as he has acknowledged, then the words that are used are symbolic and vary in meaning according to the environment and experience of man and must be interpreted and re-interpreted if they are to have relevance for the contemporary age. Baillie's chief argument has been against abstract propositions as God's revelation and, in its place, he has sought to establish a non-inferential meeting with God through personal encounter. Verbal and conceptual inspiration can end only in propositional revelation, and surely this was not the intention of Baillie when he spoke of inspiration. But he is unable to avoid this problem by his concept of verbal inspiration.

The nature of biblical authority. The Bible, Baillie believes, possesses an authority for the Christian which is all its own.[19] Although holiness is an attribute that God alone possesses, this adjective is attributed to the Scriptures because they are the vehicle through which the gospel is mediated to man. Christians today are dependent upon the Bible as the medium to bring them the witness of the apostolic community to the faith.[20] The nature of the authority of the Bible is realized for the

Christian in the purpose of the Scriptures. The purpose of the prophetic and apostolic writers was to bear witness to the redemptive activity of God. The witness which the Scripture contains seeks to lead man to an apprehension of the presence of God in Christ. The Bible is authoritative for the Christian because it is the unique prophetic and apostolic witness to the revelation of God.[21] But the authority of the Bible does not rest on an inerrant plenary view of inspiration, but on the authority of the living God who is mediated to man through the witness of the written record.

Baillie does not believe that all parts of the Bible are equally authoritative or equally inspired. He accepts Luther's criterion that the revelatory quality of each part of the Bible is to be judged according to the degree in which it "preaches Christ." All scripture is judged by the Christological criterion.[22] Portions of the Scripture become revelatory as God's spirit speaks to man through the written vehicle. Man's spirit responds to the <u>testimonium Spiritus Sancti internum</u>. As C. H. Dodd has stated: "Thus the religious authority of the Bible comes home to us primarily in inducing in us a religious attitude and outlook."[23] The Bible is not the "last word" on all theological questions, but it is the "'seminal word' out of which fresh apprehension of truth springs in the mind of man."[24]

II. THE ROLE OF LANGUAGE IN RELIGIOUS KNOWLEDGE

In the preface to the 1958 edition of <u>Our Knowledge of God,</u> Baillie states that if he were to add anything to what he had written originally in 1939, he would direct his thinking to the challenge which has come from logical atomism, logical positivism, and logical or linguistic analysis.[25] This he attempted to do in his Gifford Lectures, <u>The Sense of the Presence of God</u>. Baillie, like many contemporary theologians, has attempted to respond to the problem of theological language.

Christianity has always been concerned with language because it has always sought to make its message clear and articulate. But language as a vehicle of communication in the Christian faith has always been a means to an end and never an end in itself. The Christian Church has never been committed to words in themselves but to the living God who has revealed himself in his redemptive activity. Language is an instrumental vehicle to lead men to personal communion with God.

<u>Scripture as a medium of revelation.</u> Baillie's view of verbal inspiration has been observed, and the problems latent in it have been set forth. It was related that he rejected plenary inspiration and viewed the basic function of the Scriptures as one of witnessing to the redemptive

activity of God. This is the basic function of the Scriptures. The Scriptures always point beyond themselves to the One they are seeking to make known. The Scriptures are a medium of revelation because they bear witness to the revelation. The Scriptures are not equated with the revelation but are the medium through which the revelatory activity of God is disclosed.[26]

The essential revelation, according to Baillie, must be distinguished from the outward form. The divine revelation is always mediated intermingled with human elements, but this does not mean that the essential message of the Bible cannot be distinguished from the details of the outward form. Often the Bible is rejected because it is embedded in a particular cultural and cosmological world view. The Christian must learn to distinguish what is central and unchanging from what is peripheral truth. The criterion for judging the revelatory quality of each part of the Bible is to be found in the manner it <u>Christum treibet</u>. The essential message needs to be distinguished from the imperfections, historical inaccuracies, and conflicting reports found in the biblical record. The level of understanding revelation in the Old and New Testaments should be distinguished. When this criterion is rightly applied, a clearer understanding of the nature and inspiration of the Scriptures is determined.[27]

A proper understanding of the biblical expression "word of God" is necessary if the role of language in religious knowledge is rightly to be ascertained. Baillie observes that in the Old Testament the phrase "the word of Jahweh" occurs some four hundred times and is the most common way in the Old Testament of expressing God's revelation.[28] The meaning of this phrase cannot be limited merely to words. Greek thought made a contrast between the word and the deed, between speech and action, but Baillie notes that this is not true of the Hebrew concept. "But in Hebrew the usual word for 'word' also means an action or an event, and 'for such thought God's fiat and his effective action are one.'"[29]

The Hebrew concept of word, Baillie believes, prepared the way for the New Testament affirmation that the "Word became flesh." The "Word" of God, therefore, is never merely clothed in words but is clothed in flesh and life. The Incarnation of the <u>Logos</u> is the primary witness to the reality that God's revelation is personal and historical and not limited to communication by words. "The word of Jahweh" always comes in action and event in a personal way.[30]

The divine communion comes to the human spirit, but it is not unmediated. It is mediated by the tradition and circumstances of the prophetic and apostolic witness. The words the prophets and apostles used to describe the revelation are the vehicles used to communicate it and are not equated with it nor are they themselves the revelation. Through the medium of the Bible, however, many are led to a living encounter with God. It is in this sense, Baillie believes, that the Scriptures serve as a medium of revelation. They point to the One who is the Ultimate Reality.[31]

<u>Dialectical</u> <u>nature.</u> Following the thought of Kierkegaard, Baillie asserts that theology must always be dialectical.[32] God reveals himself to man in revelation and man responds in faith. The human concepts in which this relationship is described are always limited by finite reflection and will involve an element of paradox. Therefore, the Christian can never claim absolute certainty about the "unseen world."[33] Baillie observes that in the writings of Paul Tillich he has found many excellent statements on this aspect of thought. He quotes with apparent approval the following statement:

> To be sure, this eternal logos does pulsate through all our thinking; there can be no act of thought without the secret presupposition of its unconditional truth.
>
> But this unconditional truth is not in our possession. It is the hidden criterion of every truth that we believe we possess. There is an element of venture and of risk in every statement of truth.[34]

Baillie has gone beyond the dialectical claim by distinguishing between two kinds of knowledge, the knowledge of truth and the knowledge of reality.[35] To him, the knowledge of reality is primary, and the knowledge of truths concerning this reality is always secondary. Creeds, propositions, or theological formulations are always secondary to the experience of the reality and can never be made absolute in their description.

> The point, then, that I am most concerned to make is that, however difficult we may find it to ascribe certainty to these truths, we may nevertheless enjoy the certitude of having authentic acquaintance with the realities they fallibly seek to describe.[36]

Concerning theological formulations of the Ultimate Reality, Baillie says that man seems to be able to reach "up" to them, but he is never able to get his thought "round" them. Man's view of them is never adequate to their essential nature. He acknowledges that the "pulse of certainty" beats throughout our Christian thinking, but it is never captured in finite formulations. God is never known <u>per se</u> but only <u>quod nos</u>; he is the <u>deus revelatus</u> that is always the <u>deus absconditus</u>. God's nature is always clouded in mystery, and though man may not have perfect knowledge of the infinite, he has sufficient light to illumine his way so that he can follow the will of God.37

<u>Religious knowledge as symbolical.</u> When revelation takes place, Baillie believes that man's reflective analysis entails problems with his way of knowing and with the content of the knowledge itself. Revelation occurs only within a personal relationship. The revelation from the divine mind to the human is different from the revelation of one human mind to another. The attempt to describe how one person knows another is difficult, but Baillie believes that an analysis of how one knows God is deeply mysterious. An attempt to describe a friend's personality, mind or character is reduced to trying to describe some of his qualities or to relate some of his words or actions, but, in no sense, can the description be exhaustive. The listener may grasp something of the man, but this will be true only because the friend's personality is analogous with other personalities that are known. A friend's qualities may be described in a number of abstract nouns, but the abstraction cannot exhaust the fullness of his personality. Each abstract noun half reveals and half conceals the personality within.38

These same considerations apply, in Baillie's opinion, in greater intensity to God's revelation to man. An exhaustive account can never be given of the ways man knows God or of the God that is known. God is not like a friend, who is one person among many, but he is the source of all the universe. Although man is limited in his relations with others by his psychosomatic organization, there is nothing which cannot serve as a medium for God's revelation. No abstract nouns or enumeration of attributes, however, can exhaustively enclose the infinite richness of the divine personality.39

There is a true sense in which all human thoughts about God are involved in an unavoidable symbolism. This is depicted by Baillie in the following passage:

> Furthermore, it is certain that none of our human thoughts of the Divine can ever be wholly adequate to their infinite object. What God is in Himself must ever remain unimaginable to finite minds, and ineffable to finite lips. We cannot hope that any thought or word of ours should hold His whole Being in its grasp; the highest task we can set ourselves is only to discover which

aspects of our poor human experience afford us the least misleading clue to the transcendence of His glory. To forget this is not merely bad philosophy, it is bad religion; for true religion has always taught that His ways are not as our ways but are past finding out.[40]

Baillie is not, however, willing to state that all theological statements are symbolical in nature. He realizes that in the "widest sense" all terms are symbolic, but he feels that its theological usage must be defined a little more narrowly than it is used in everyday speech. Theological symbolism is defined by him "as a way of thinking and speaking which, while pointing to the infinite, the divine and the unseen, describes it in terms of things seen, human and finite."[41] Differing with Tillich, who believes that everything man says about God is symbolic except the statement about "being itself," Baillie states that he cannot accept the position which depicts all of man's knowledge of God as being reached by analogy from man's experience of the finite world. In the affirmation that God is personal, he believes that man is making an intelligible assertion. Divine personality is not a symbol that points beyond itself but is perfect personality. The infinite cannot be reached by an extension of finite series.[42]

In Baillie's thinking there is an element of truth in the doctrine of the *analogia entis*. He rejects the Aristotelian and Thomistic forms and follows the Platonic form advanced by Bonaventure.[43] In this interpretation of the *analogia entis*, the knowledge of God comes to man in conjunction with his knowledge of his fellow man, but it is not dependent upon it. He expresses this in the following way:

> What is true in the doctrine of the *analogia entis* is that the knowledge of God does not precede our knowledge of man in time but is given "in, with and under" such knowledge, and that therefore no one of God's attributes is ever given to us save in conjunction with--that is, in comparison with and in contrast to--some corresponding attribute of man. What is false is the assumption that the comparison moves from man to God instead of from God to man. Such a view, if consistently carried out, is bound to end in anthropomorphism, that is, in a breach of the second commandment.[44]

This position is consistent with Baillie's view that man's knowledge of God is mediated to him through finite realities; it is also compatible with his position that the divine is never reached by inference, even if the inference is analogical in character. This would take the initiative away from God and posit it in the mind of the creature. This view Baillie has always rejected.[45]

Later in his discussion, Baillie begins to confront the problem of trying to analyze which theological statements are non-symbolic. In relation to God are good, holy, eternal, infinite, spirit, and father non-symbolic? This is what Baillie has sought to expound, but it does not seem thoroughly convincing. Baillie's interpretation of the <u>analogia</u> <u>entis</u> is well taken, but his unwillingness to see the symbolic nature of man's interpretation of the encounter presents problems. Knowledge of God does not arise by inference about God from a finite creature, but when God has taken the initiative and has revealed himself to man, is man able to describe this in any way other than by non-symbolic language?

In speaking of God as personal, Baillie favors the Platonic view in which God is depicted as both the form and a soul. God is envisioned as both being and existence, universal and yet concretely personal.[46] God is a person in a non-symbolic way. But can the term person be made literally applicable to God? Does not this term arise in and through the encounter with God, and is it not attributed to him because it is the highest reality of which man is cognizant? God is spoken of as personal within the Scriptures, still this does not mean that God is a person beside others. Although God is doubtless far greater than the best we know, he cannot be less. God is of course ultimate reality, but can man speak of this ultimate reality in any way other than in changing symbolic categories? Non-symbolic language is certainly inadequate to open up levels of reality that are beyond the grasp of man. The various biblical categories, ideas, metaphors, and interpretations are symbolic in the sense that they point beyond themselves to the ultimate reality. Religious symbols must become transparent and not be seen in themselves but seen only as witnesses to the revelation.

Whenever religious symbols replace that to which they are supposed to point, they become idols. Idolatry is the absolutizing of the symbols of the Holy and making them identical with the Holy itself. The biblical witness can never contain the reality to which it points because its purpose is that of witness. A man witnesses to that which has grasped him ultimately, but his interpretation, even the apostolic witness, can never be absolutized because it can only be expressed in symbolic language which must be interpreted anew to each generation. Baillie himself acknowledges that man must avoid worshiping the medium of revelation. "Bibliolatry is to be avoided because the Biblical documents are fallible and because we must not worship what is fallible."[47]

Baillie has stated that the knowledge of reality is primary and the knowledge of the truths concerning this reality secondary, nevertheless, man is aware that he has authentic acquaintance with reality.[48] The vehicle may not be perfect, but it directs man to the ultimate. "The pulse of certainty beats throughout the whole of our Christian knowledge, but we can never quite capture it for our particular formulations."[49]

III. THE VERIFICATION OF RELIGIOUS KNOWLEDGE

It has already been noted that one of Baillie's intentions in writing The Sense of the Presence of God was to confront the impact of logical positivism and linguistic analysis on religious knowledge.[50] He has endeavored to establish a "sort of general" knowledge of God against the exclusive emphasis of Barth's Christocentricism and at the same time maintain the uniqueness of Christianity on a cognitive basis. In order to do this, he has had to come to grips with both the Barthian and the logical empirical positions. Baillie's analysis of the Barthian perspective was examined earlier, and now his approach to the question of verification will be considered.

Truth and relevance. Baillie has clearly indicated in his response to the logical positivists and linguistic analysts that the moral relevance of a doctrine is the significant factor to him and not the contrast between meaning or use. In adopting the "use-principle," he follows R. B. Braithwaite, a logical empiricist who teaches at Cambridge, and asserts that "moral statements have a use in guiding conduct; and if they have a use they surely have a meaning in some sense of meaning."[51] Baillie's utilization of the "use-principle" is a limited and special kind which places the emphasis on the practical conduct of living and which acknowledges the use of Christian affirmations as they contribute to the frame of reference which serves for guidance in Christian living.

> The two things I want to say, then, are that no affirmation has right of place within a system of Christian theology if it has no such usefulness, and that the meaning of any such affirmation is best understood from an examination of the precise difference it would make to the conduct of Christian life if it were not believed or at least if it were deliberately denied.[52]

The chief concern of Baillie with doctrine bears not on its truth but in its relevance. John Macmurray, a British philosopher, has influenced him convincingly on this perspective. All theory, he believes, must find verification in action because all meaningful knowledge is for the sake of action. If one is aware of the difference it would make in his intentions if he acted as though a particular proposition were true, then the proposition has meaning. The practical difference for moral living is the significant factor.

> My own contention then is that no doctrine has right of place within our Christian theology unless we can show that the denial of it would disturb or distort the pattern of our Christian sharing in the koinonia of agapé which goes back to Pentecost and which I have described as a triangular system of relationships between the triune God, ourselves and our fellows.[53]

Nature of verification. With the rise of the philosophy of linguistic analysis around the beginning of the twentieth century, such men as Ludwig Wittgenstein, Rudolf Carnap, A. J. Ayer and others have urged that the obscurity of language be classified by the use of a principle which has come to be noted as the "verification principle." Verificational analysts claim that no knowledge can be accepted as true unless it is capable of verification in terms of sense experience. This school of thought has ruled that practically all Christian theological statements are meaningless because they cannot be verified in terms of sense experience.[54]

In discussing the philosophy of linguistic analysis, Baillie observes that the modern empiricist is a behaviourist in his psychology, a subjectivist in his ethics and aesthetics, and an agnostic in his attitude toward religion. When the empiricist states that there can be no knowledge except that which is established on the evidence of bodily sense, he is saying either that man can have no knowledge of any reality unless it is corporeal in nature, or that any non-corporeal knowledge of reality is established by inference from observing the corporeal. Baillie observes that the empiricists today hold that the only direct knowledge one has is his own bodily selfhood, therefore, analogy is impossible since inference cannot be made from non-corporeal existence.[55] This, he believes, leads to a strange result. "Since all reality is corporeal, the knower is as corporeal as the things he knows. But how can body know body? Only if knowledge is itself body."[56]

Baillie notes that the empiricist believes that veridical knowledge is derived from experience and can be verified by reference to it. He differs with the linguistic philosophy that seeks to reduce experience to the corporeal. He contends that there is a "sense" experience of things other than the corporeal. "The human spirit, I shall say, develops certain subtler senses or sensitivities which go beyond the bodily senses."[57]

Reference is made to Newman's "illative sense," and to the familiar references such as a sense of beauty, sense of duty, sense of humor, sense of honor, a sense of the holy or a sense of the presence of God. These, he acknowledges, presuppose the experience acquired through bodily senses, but, nevertheless, they go beyond the corporeal sense and bring an awareness of aspects of reality which could not be experienced otherwise. This sense enables one to "perceive something not otherwise perceptible" instead of merely conceiving it as a concept which has been reached by argument.[58] This is what Baillie calls the "non-sensuous perception."[59]

Alfred Jules Ayer, a proponent of the logical empirical approach, has insisted that "every factual proposition must refer to sense-experience."[60] But in the same work he has stated: "It should be clear that there are no absolutely certain empirical propositions. It is only tautologies that are certain."[61] However, this statement by Ayer is certainly not a tautology. How can he be so certain of it? Baillie believes that instead of verifying ethical, aesthetic, and religious knowledge on the corporeal level, they should be verifiable on their own level.

> But against this I would submit that, whereas indeed our ethical, aesthetic and religious knowledge is capable of verification and should constantly be subjected to such, this must be carried out by a return, not to our experience of corporeal reality, but, as the case may be, to our ethical, aesthetic or religious experience itself.[62]

In Baillie's opinion, all true judgments of value are capable of logical justification, but he does not believe that it is through analytic reasoning that the truth is first apprehended. A musical theorist may give reasons why Beethoven's symphony is more beautiful than an orchestral "Selection" from the latest musical comedy. But if one prefers the musical comedy after hearing both, will he be convinced even if the true laws of melody and counterpoint are presented to him? One can only hope that a larger and wider musical experience will direct him to a deeper insight into music appreciation. How does one determine the method by which he will verify a judgment that a piece of music is beautiful? Since music theory is drawn from musical experience and from no other area, it can be verified in no other way than by an appeal to the self-same experience. It is verifiable by reference only to the experience out of which it emerged.[63]

This same principle is applied to theological judgments. "Theological judgments can be verified only by a return to the area of primary apprehension which we call faith."[64] For the verification or falsification of a theological judgment, one must refer to faith's primary apprehension of the divine.

> Just as there is no way of developing a juster (sic) sense of what is excellent in poetry except by living with poetry, by hearing and reading more and more of it, so there is no way of deepening and refining our faith, save by living the life of faith, which is the same as to say by being more humbly open to receive, and more diligently prepared to attend to, what is being divinely revealed to us.[65]

Baillie does not acknowledge that theology can be placed on the same level with science to demonstrate the fundamental validity of the religious conscience and the truth of its affirmations.[66] In fact, he does not believe that even natural science can discover, by empirical methods, the purpose in nature.[67] Religion is at the opposite scale from such an analytical field as geometry. Are there really any philosophical systems that are not built on assumptions or presuppositions that can be demonstrated by empirical means? Baillie believes that there are none. Beginning with Aristotle and noting various philosophers, he attempts to show that every science begins with certain beliefs which it assumes and does not attempt to prove.[68] The great logician, F. H. Bradley, was aware that logical inference is always a construction followed by an intuition.[69]

In the book <u>Philosophy in a New Key</u>, Susanne Langer has demonstrated that all mental activity begins in some sort of "symbolic transformation." Applying this principle to logical empiricism, she has observed that the error of this philosophical approach is its failure to recognize that even its discursive propositions were the result of a process of symbolic transformation. The logical empiricists have overlooked an important step in the mental formulation of sense data. Langer has attempted to expose the logical structure that lies behind the propositions. She has examined the complexities involved in language itself. The modes of ritual, myth, and music were distinguished from language itself by her as being "nondiscursive" or "presentational" modes of symbolism. Her conclusion is that all thought and knowledge proceeds from "symbolic transformation" and becomes discursive only at an advanced point in its formulation.[70]

Brian Gerrish has stated that the "verification principle" has been criticized by various philosophers and has been made obsolete by the total revision by Ludwig Wittgenstein of his own theory of language. He notes that in his latter work, <u>Philosophical Investigation</u>, Wittgenstein has stated that one is not to ask for meaning but for the use of words and that every statement has its own logic. The truth here is that logic of statements about God may not have the same logic as statements about tables, chairs, rabbits, or sputniks. When the concern is with theological assertions, then one must be aware of the rules that determine the use of theological statements.[71] In acknowledging that the old style positivism of the Vienna Circle is dead, Gerrish makes the following interesting observation:

> The old belligerance (sic) of the Vienna Circle has, then, been transmuted into a mild interrogative: should we come across a stray positivist who has not yet purchased a copy of Wittgenstein's Investigations, we would know how to deal with him. We must do two things; first admit to him that we cannot offer the kind of verification he demands; then, insist that what he demands is unreasonable. We must show him that not all statements are used to make verifiable assertions (in his narrow sense of the term "verifiable"); and if he refuses to allow meaning to any other statements than verifiable assertions, we must show him that his theory of meaning is outmoded--must show him, in fact, that he is guilty of bigotry, conservatism, and most of the other things which he accuses us of.[72]

Elton Trueblood has touched the vulnerable point of logical positivism when he noted that the very premise upon which the positivists begin cannot be verified according to their own principle of verification. The basic proposition of logical positivism is that "no statement of fact is meaningful unless it can be verified in sense experience." He then asks, "how does the positivist determine the truth or credibility of this proposition?" According to the philosophy of the positivists, only two types of statements are true. These two are the strictly logical and those determined by sense experience. But this fundamental proposition can be verified by neither of the two types which they allow. Instead of being empirical, as they claim it is, the position of the logical positivists is one of arbitrary dogmatism.[73]

The position of Gerrish is close to Baillie's own thought. Baillie has insisted that a statement can be verified only by returning to the area of experience out of which it arose. No one can arbitrarily set up a principle and demand that all areas of experience are verifiable by it alone. The grounds for certitude can never be reduced to sense data. Man's ethical, aesthetic, and religious knowledge is capable of verification, as Baillie has observed, but this verification should be administered not by a return to corporeal reality, but by returning to the region of experience out of which it emerged. The type of certainty that the logical positivists desire is not possible in religious faith. As Tillich has said:

> Revelation claims to give a truth which is both certain and of ultimate concern--a truth which includes and accepts the risk and uncertainty of every significant cognitive act, yet transcends it in accepting it.74

Criterion of revelation. What then is the criterion for judging the truth or falsification of any claim to revelation? Baillie declares that the verification or falsification of revelation is determined by the faith's primary apprehension of the divine. The faith of which Baillie speaks here is the single apprehension or the single illumination of the believing mind. Faith is a trustful commitment to the primary reality.75 In what way can it be tested? He answers this question in the following manner:

> It would appear that the veridical nature of any primary mode of apprehension cannot be tested by reference to anything outside itself. Each must carry its own witness or must collapse. If the trust we repose in it be not self-authenticating, there is no other apparent way of authenticating it.76

Religious faith has its own ordo cognoscendi.77 In Baillie's belief, it is impossible to separate the question of the criterion of truth and falsity in religion from the question of religion's inmost essence. In answering one of these questions, the other is answered at the same time. Religious truth is not capable of being reduced to any totally non-religious premises.78 "Religions can be tested only from within."79 Whether they are judged as high or low, adequate or inadequate, true or false, must be determined Baillie states:

> In accordance with the extent to which they are true to their own central principle--the root idea for which all religion stands; or, more accurately, in accordance with the adequacy with which they positively express and expand that principle.80

A claim to revelation is rationally tested by its ability to fulfill its own premises. This is to affirm that one cannot judge a claim to revelation by standards that are established apart from revelation. To test Christian revelation by some standard apart from the revelation itself, is to make that standard the ultimate ground of faith and subject to no rational test itself. If Christ is the fullness of the revelation of the truth of God, then all revelation must be judged by his unique revelation.[81]

CHAPTER V

THE PRACTICAL AFFIRMATION OF RELIGIOUS KNOWLEDGE

All religious knowledge, Baillie believes, must find verification in action. Religious knowledge has no meaning apart from the practical aspect of daily living. Man's religious knowledge is never an isolated affair but finds its inception in the community of faith and is meaningful only as it is understood in its consciousness of others. Religious knowledge and morality, therefore, cannot be divorced. The practical affirmation of religious knowledge is veritably one of Baillie's chief emphases.

I. THE CHRISTIAN FRAME OF REFERENCE

The Christian faith is understood by Baillie as a "frame of reference" which will enable the believer to respond appropriately to every circumstance of life. The Christian faith is a system of "co-ordinates" within which the believer lives and acts as he responds to every situation of life.

> He knows now how to assess the relative authority of the multitudinous claims that are made upon him from every side, and how to meet each. He knows now how best to spend his time, and also how best to spend his money, believing himself to hold both only in stewardship to a higher authority. He knows how to face what we call the buffetings of fortune--disappointment, suspense, unrequited love, frustrated ambition, accident, bereavement and all the rest. He knows how to take pain and sickness, and in particular how to think of "the last enemy" and how to meet it when it comes. But he knows no less how to enjoy the good things of life, how to comport himself in calm weather as well as in the storm, and how to play as well as to work.[1]

The Gospel. In order to understand the Christian frame of reference, Baillie thinks that one needs to be aware of how the frame of reference originated. The early Christians firmly believed that their faith was rooted in the tradition of their Hebrew forefathers. But, nevertheless, they believed that something new had been revealed in the Gospel. The Gospel is the crown and completion of the Old Testament teaching and radically fulfills its expectation. The Christians believed, however, that the Old Testament can be rightly understood only in the light of the New

Testament. The Old Testament is understood through the illumination which has come in the Gospel, and the Gospel is the standard for judging the Old Testament or the sacred books of pagan religions.[2]

The Gospel is the good news of God's activity. The <u>Kerygma</u> is the proclamation that the <u>kairos</u> has come in Jesus Christ. The Gospel is the good news that God has given himself to man in communion. Baillie believes that two things are implied in this concept of communion. The first thing implied is that God's revelation is fundamentally personal and not propositional. The second implication is that God reveals himself in action within history.[3] The Bible is essentially a record of the Acts of God. The Mosaic law in all its prescriptions is predicated upon the covenant between Yahweh and Israel. Throughout the Old Testament the divine activity of God's saving action is declared in the law, the poetic works, and prophetic writings. God's activity was realized by the interpreters as being definite and historical. Yahweh is understood by Baillie as the personal God who has revealed himself within historical events to Abraham, Isaac, and Jacob.[4]

The New Testament bears witness to a revelation through events. The Gospel is the announcement or proclamation of the good news of what God has accomplished in history through Jesus Christ. Jesus was not merely announcing an event which would take place independently of him, but his very coming was the event of which he was proclaiming. The Gospel is understood correctly in terms of <u>Heilsgeschichte</u>, the redemptive activity of God.[5] Acts 10:39-43, which is a portion of Peter's sermon preached in the home of Cornelius, is, according to Baillie, "the whole Gospel in a nutshell."[6] It is the declaration of what God has done in Christ.

<u>A way of life</u>. In realizing that the Gospel is concerned with declaring the redemptive activity of God, Baillie notes that the word used to describe man's deliverance is life, $\zeta \omega \acute{\eta}$. Life is the New Testament word used most often to describe God's deliverance of sinful man. Baillie quotes more than fourteen passages from the Scriptures that denote Christ as the life and the one in whom is found deliverance from the human exigencies of sin and death. The way of life is revealed in Christ because God has revealed himself through him.[7]

Since the early Christians were aware that life was found in Christ, they became known as followers of Jesus or men of the way of Jesus. Long before the Christians were called by that name they were spoken of as men of the way or men of the road.[8] By this, the Christians sought to designate that they were followers of Christ in the way that he had lived, the way of the cross. "Christianity, then," Baillie believes, "is a way of living, which includes a way of thinking, a way of feeling and a way of behaving."[9] The Christian way is described in the New Testament in terms of koinōnia and agapé. The Greek word κοιγωνία is translated into the English words of fellowship, community, and communion. A Christian is one who shares in this fellowship. Ἀγάπη is the Greek word for love which is virtually inexpressible in English. It denotes the God-like love which has come from the divine and which the Christians are to direct toward their fellow man. The Christian way is understood by Baillie to be "the way followed within the koinōnia of agapé."[10]

The characteristic life of the Christian koinōnia is understood in terms of a triangular relationship. In this relationship there is man himself, his fellow Christian, and God as he has been revealed in Christ. This triangular relationship is such that a second angle can only be reached by way of the third. God can be reached and loved only through one's neighbor, and, at the same time, God does not reach man or manifest his love apart from one's fellow man.[11] Here again Baillie has emphasized his view of the mediated immediacy. Man's knowledge of God always comes in conjunction with his knowledge of others. He believes that the knowledge of God is not given to those who are not involved in the service of their fellow man. The knowledge of God comes to a person individually but never in isolation. This fact affirms the necessity of the fellowship of the Church and denotes the rejection of religious individualism. In this sense Baillie believes that the Cyprianic formula, extra ecclesiam nulla salus, is true.[12]

> There is therefore great need today for laying fresh emphasis upon the doctrine of the Church . . . . We must correct the widespread notion that Christianity is merely an individual affair of the individual soul . . . . We must, therefore, teach men afresh that the blessings of the Gospel cannot be enjoyed by the single individual in his singleness, but only in his incorporation into Christ's Mystical Body, the Holy Catholic Church.[13]

The agapeistic way of life can be expressed only in conjunction with others. Man's love for God can find effective expression only in love toward his fellow man. Baillie believes that the Cyprianic formula can correctly be translated as " 'the man who keeps to himself cannot be made whole.' "[14] The unity of mankind is as much a truth of Christianity as the doctrine of the unity of God.[15] Man returns God's love when he serves his neighbor. In understanding Christianity as a way of life, Baillie does not believe that this reduces it to mere morality. In fact, he does not believe that a distinction can be made between religion and morality.

Morality cannot be separated from religion. All authentically Christian thinking does not only issue in action but is for the sake of action. Christian action which is directed toward others is not a separate thing from Christian action toward God, but is the only genuine way of serving God in the way of love.[16]

Baillie's thinking concerning the solidarity of mankind certainly has a note of realism about it. Man does indeed experience God personally, but with this experience there always has to be the realization of man's solidaristic involvement with humanity. Man is never an atomistic individual in his relationship with God; he stands within the commonwealth of humanity. Since the life of humanity is infinitely interwoven, no personal religious experience that does not have in it a relationship to one's fellow man can be a distinctively Christian experience. Faith is indeed an intensely personal matter, but it can never be merely a private matter because man is never an isolated ego. J. S. Whale points this out when he says:

> Indeed, the most private act that any man can perform is to die, to go out of life. As long as he is alive at all he cannot and does not live unto himself. Personality is mutual in its very being. For all its sovereign individuality, the self exists only in a community of selves. The lonely Robinson Crusoe is a possible fiction because he begins as a man before becoming a solitary; but the lonely Tarzan of the Apes is an impossible fiction because he begins as a solitary before coming a man. Society is only the aggregate of individual selves, admittedly; yet individual selfhood is achieved only in society. In one sense, therefore, the part is prior to the whole: but in another sense the whole is prior to the part. In short, human life demands to be understood in terms of its two complementary aspects, the individual and the corporate, the part and the whole. Each has to be interpreted in terms of the other.[17]

The reign of God. In his discussion of the Christian frame of reference, Baillie alludes to the fact that the reign of God was central in much of the teaching of Jesus. Baillie prefers the phrase, reign of God, instead of Kingdom of God because, he believes, that the former phrase refers to "an administration rather than a realm, and a time rather than a place."[18] He is aware of the ambiguity that surrounds the concept of the reign of God. But he wants to emphasize the fact that in some sense the Christian is living in the new age, although he awaits in expectation for the fulfillment or the consummation of the age. In a sense the Christian lives in both ages at once. The reign of God is both a present reality and a future reality for whose consummation the Church awaits.[19]

In the Christ-event a new era has been inaugurated. The Christ-event is the paradigmatic experience which issued at Pentecost in the fellowship of Christian love. "It provides the paradigm in the light of which all other events are to be interpreted, the frame of reference within which they are to be set."[20] The Christian frame of reference is centered primarily in the Christ-event which gives significance to all other encounters of life whether they are past, present or future. The Christ-event provides the paradigm to which every reality in the world and in history is related in some way to this central fact.[21] The Christian frame of reference is realized in the Christ-event. This event becomes the focal point of history. Baillie's acknowledgement of Christ as the paradigm of all of life is surely a principle to which he subscribes by faith. It is a view that is predicated on his belief and experience of what Jesus in reality was and what he accomplished and what in reality he is and continues to do. With an emphasis on the Incarnational nature of God's redemptive activity, Baillie states that "the fullness of revelation is only in Jesus Christ, and in Him all other revelation is comprehended and summed up."[22] In this sense, he truly becomes the paradigm by which all of life is measured.

The Christian hope. In one of his addresses, Baillie observes that many of the most penetrating contemporary writers have given way largely to disenchantment and that a spirit of hopelessness has begun to overwhelm the outlook of humanity. In the realization of the pessimistic mood, he directs man to the Christian faith in order to see what it has to say concerning hope and despair.[23] In his book, And the Life Everlasting, Baillie seeks to show that the Christian does have hope, hope not only in the present life but in the life to come. The Christian's hope is based on his personal knowledge of the eternal God. The Christian hope is rooted in man's religious fellowship with God.[24] Man's hope of eternal life issues out of his awareness that he can have knowledge of God in communion with him.

The only unanswerable argument for immortality, Baillie believes, is realized in the fact that God is the God of individuals who can enter into fellowship with him. Here he sets forth his "logic of hope." "If the individual can commune with God, then he must matter to God; and if he matters to God, he must share God's eternity."[25] The Christian hope of eternal life is grounded in man's fellowship with God. Baillie has set forth his grounds for the Christian hope of eternal life in the form of what he has called "the logic of hope." His major premise is predicated on the reality of God which comes through man's experience of fellowship with

God. The experience of religion has place in a man's life when God reveals himself to man and man responds by putting his trust in God. Religion in its highest embodiment becomes the experience of the love of God. God reveals himself to man as one who loves him and who is omnipotent in his power. Nothing less than one who is infinite in his love and power could be worthy of worship.26

The minor premise of hope's syllogism is an ethical proposition. "Something of intrinsic value resides in human individuality."27 Baillie believes that the distinction between theology and ethics, however, is not a valid one. He would, therefore, affirm that the souls of men are precious to God. The question of values entails a theological perspective as well as an ethical one. Baillie dismisses the attempts to deny this premise by reducing its significance to the immortality of influence or the immortality of the race. He also asserts that it is invalid to speak of man as being lost in "reabsorption" into the spiritual being. He believes that one cannot retain personality in God unless it is also retained in man. If a man's personality may disappear at death without anything of significance being lost, then why would man not be absolved of respecting his fellow man's personality in the present?28

It is of the utmost importance, Baillie believes, that those who deny the conclusion of hope's syllogism make clear which of the two premises they doubt. He points out what the denial of each premise will entail in the following statement:

> Every one who denies the doctrine of personal immortality is denying either the ultimate conservation by the universe of the values that emerge during its process or the intrinsic nature of the value that resides in personality. Either he is doubting the reality of God the Father Almighty or he is holding it possible that God should will the annihilation of the souls He loves--or at the very least the dissipation of their individualities.29

Baillie's argument for immortality is based not on explicit logic which those outside the household of faith are likely to accept, but it is founded instead on an implicit logic which will be more convincing to those who are committed to the Christ-like way. The way to attain a surer hope, he believes, is not by argumentative means, but by a deeper human experience of fellowship with God and love toward one's fellow man. Man's hope for immortality issues from his knowledge of God and the significance of individual personality which man acknowledges as precious by his attitude of love toward others.

II. RELIGIOUS KNOWLEDGE AND MORALITY

All religious theory, Baillie believes, if it is meaningful, must find verification in action. All meaningful religious knowledge is for the sake of action. In the last chapter it was observed that Baillie believes that the moral relevance of doctrine is the significant factor. His utilization of the "use-principle" is a limited and special kind which places the emphasis on the practical conduct of living. Christian affirmations are meaningful if they contribute to the frame of reference which serves for guidance in Christian living.[30] Religious knowledge and morality are bound together. Man is involved in a triangular system of relationships between God, himself, and his fellow man. Religious knowledge of God for man finds its genuine inception and relevance in the moral realm.

<u>Consciousness of value.</u> In many of his books, and especially in his earlier ones, Baillie has placed a heavy emphasis on the significance of the consciousness of value. Here he reveals his indebtedness to Herrmann and Kant. He maintains that the consciousness of value is itself a religious experience. He affirms his belief in the organic nature of the relation between faith and morals. In man's apprehension of value, he is being apprehended by God.[31] In his definition of religion, he has stated that "<u>religion is a moral trust in reality.</u>"[32] Religion arises through man's moral values as he is apprehended by Divine Reality. In another work, he has given a similar definition:

> Shall we say that <u>religious faith is a consciousness which comes to the dutiful, to the loyal, to those who seek after the highest values they know, that in being thus dutiful and loyal to their values, they are doing what they were meant and appointed to do, and are putting themselves in line with the Eternal and have His backing behind them</u>?[33]

The roots of religion are in man's consciousness of value. It is an outlook which arises out of one's effort to do his duty. But religion has greater depth than a consciousness of value or the love of goodness because it is concerned ultimately with the relation of value to reality. The Socratic and Platonic influences, as well as the influence of one of his teachers, Andrew Seth Pringle-Pattison, are apparent in Baillie's thought here. The relation of value to reality is expressed in the identity of goodness and being, and the worship of the ideal conceived as the eternal real. This is what Baillie has described as the "headwaters of world-religion." A great sense of trust in an Eternal Goodness is acquired by those who seek goodness in life. This, Baillie declares, is one of the best established facts of history.34

The agapeistic way of love is the highest known value which has been revealed by God. This is the distinctive feature of Christianity. In the outlook of Jesus toward life man was enabled to see that the law of love gave genuine meaning to life. Through the revelation in Christ, "the law of loving-kindness was realised in its full meaning and made to cover every relationship of life."35

Even in his earliest discussions of the consciousness of value, Baillie does not believe that reality is arrived at by inference from these values. Man's sense of values is not understood as something that he has acquired by his own initiative but belongs to the progressive disclosure of the higher order of ultimate reality.36 The Kantian categorical imperative is exceeded by Baillie when he declares that the moral consciousness refers to a living person and not merely to an impersonal moral law.37 He argues that the source of the moral obligation is the living God himself who is directly revealed.

> The real truth is not that man at last concludes that his values imply the reality of God, but rather that from the beginning he <u>finds God in his values</u>. And it is God himself that he finds, and no mere reflection of Him. Love is not merely like God, but in a real sense is God.38

<u>The moral argument for theism</u>. In some of his earlier works Baillie has sought to demonstrate that the real argument for theism is based on moral considerations.39 Baillie was convinced that the moral argument was the real ground upon which the thought of Plato, Spinoza, Kant, and Jesus himself was founded. The subtitle of one of his early articles was entitled: "A Plea For a Reconsideration of the Kantian Ethic."40 According to Baillie, the fundamental source of all truly religious belief in God is predicated upon the awareness that man is unable to understand the real meaning of life in terms of moral values without supposing the existence of God. Although he believes that all true judgments of value are capable of logical justification, he does not adhere to the view that they can be apprehended by means of analytic reasoning.41 No artificial criterion can be established for unification, however. In the last chapter Baillie's position on this principle was noted; and it was observed that all judgments, including those of value, must be verified on their own level. He maintains that values are intuited before they are understood, and men are led into an awareness of God's reality, not by irrefragable arguments, but by the perception of moral values which are grounded in ultimate reality. Although man is unable to articulate the reasons for

his experience, he is aware that it is real. Realizing that exact reasoning to express this experience is hard to state, Baillie quotes with agreement the famous words from Pascal: "La coeur a ses raisons, que la raison ne connaît pas."[42]

Belief and morality. Although Baillie's emphasis on the consciousness of value was stressed with great force in his earlier works, this does not mean that it is totally absent from his later works. The emphasis in his later works, like Our Knowledge of God and The Sense of the Presence of God, is on the divine initiative which ushers in the obligation and practical application to life of the encounter one has had with the Absolute. Man is aware of the sense of the presence of God who has encountered him personally. Out of this personal encounter arises man's sense of obligation and way of life.[43]

Baillie does not identify God with duty or religion with morality, although he has been accused of this.[44] H. D. Lewis is correct, in the writer's opinion, in noting that more must be involved in a belief in God than "an uneasy conscience." The writer has also criticized Baillie's view at this very point.[45] But Baillie has affirmed that religion differs from morality precisely in that it always exhibits a transcendental reference. This transcendental reference is beyond human society and finite purpose and is grounded in the eternal purpose of the personal God.[46]

The element of belief is important because it is based on convictions without which religion would lapse into pure morality. In Chapter III it was observed that Baillie does not advocate a "formless" faith. He believes that man's knowledge of God is personal and immediate and not inferential; but he declares that man's knowledge about God is an outgrowth of this encounter. He is anxious to establish the primacy of trust over assent. But in this trust there is presupposed a necessary acquaintance with its object and latently an assent to certain affirmations that can be made about that object. Man could not put his trust in a God that he does not believe to exist or whom he believes is not worthy of the confidence placed in him. Baillie states that man cannot be convinced that he needs to be good without believing certain things about the moral nature of God.

> To retain the ethical idealism and ethical aspirations of Christianity while giving up its faith in God; to believe that I must be good without believing either that God is good or that He wants me to be good--that is not a course which it is logically open for anybody to take. There is in my own mind no shadow of doubt that Christianity has been right in asserting that moral obligation cannot mean

anything apart from belief in a divine Goodness at the heart of things; my mind is beset with many doubts about traditional Christianity, but not with that one.[47]

To center the personal encounter of God with man in the consciousness of value seems to be a predication well founded. No rational creature is totally void of moral experience. All rational creatures are cognizant of the difference between right and wrong. Although environmental, social or personal factors might obscure what that difference is, moral philosophers are agreed that there is a distinction. The moral challenge that man experiences in his consciousness of value is not distinct from God, but it is God himself who is challenging man. Man does not experience God and then infer the moral demand from that encounter; nor does man respond to the moral claim and then encounter God. Man encounters God in and with the moral claim that is being made upon him. Morality and the knowledge of God are indissoluble. This fact is clearly discernible within the Scriptures and life.

<u>The inseparability of religion and morality</u>. The spiritual solidarity of man and his moral involvement with his fellow man seem to have been axiomatic social principles in the mind of Jesus. Religion and morality can never be separated. Man's life can reflect love toward God only in unselfish love toward his fellow man. Two passages from the New Testament will serve to illustrate this point.

> Then the King will say to those at his right hand, "Come, O blessed of my Father, inherit the kingdom prepared for you from the foundation of the world; for I was hungry and you gave me food, I was thirsty and you gave me drink, I was a stranger and you welcomed me, I was naked and you clothed me, I was sick and you visited me, I was in prison and you came to me." Then the righteous will answer him, "Lord, when did we see thee hungry and feed thee, or thirsty and give thee drink? And when did we see thee a stranger and welcome thee, or naked and clothe thee? And when did we see thee sick or in prison and visit thee?" And the King will answer them, "Truly I say to you, as you did it to one of the least of these my brethren, you did it to me."[48]

In the Johannine epistle the following statement is descriptive of man's love toward God:

> If any one says, "I love God," and hates his brother, he

> is a liar; for he who does not love his brother whom he has seen, cannot love God whom he has not seen. And this commandment we have from him, that he who loves God should love his brother also.[49]

The witness of the Scriptures is that this insight of conjunctive love between man and God and between man and man goes back to the revelation of God himself through Jesus. Baillie's position seems well founded, then, when he depicts man's relationship with God as being predicated on a triangular relationship involving the self, others, and God.[50] Man's most effective expression of his love of God is realized in his love for his neighbor. Not being an isolated ego, man expresses his love in actuality only in community with others. All Christian thinking must issue in action if it is to have any real significance.[51] This action is engendered in and through the moral experience where man encounters God.

Practical and regulative. The practical and regulative aspects of man's religious knowledge are distinguished from the theoretical and speculative. Baillie has examined the theoretical and speculative side of religious knowledge, but he is convinced that all meaningful knowledge is for the sake of action. It is not enough to rest in the abstract and speculative. The knowledge of God is meaningful only if it begets action; religious knowledge must issue in morality.[52]

The guide for the practical aspect of religious knowledge is based on the Christian frame of reference, which has been discussed above. The Christ-event provides the paradigm for the regulative aspect of life. The Christian draws his example, his hope, and guidance for his daily conduct from the paradigmatic experience of the Christ.[53]

Religious knowledge which is grounded in a consciousness of value has as its distinguishing mark the characteristic of being relevant for man's ultimate ends of desire and action.

> And that is the same as to say that it is relevant to our ethical ends, and that no knowledge or belief can be regarded as authentically religious in character unless it possesses this ethical relevance.[54]

The truth of Christianity must be demonstrable in man's daily walk and conversation. The Christian truth must be worked out in practice in the lives of those who follow the living Christ.[55] Baillie follows Kant in stressing that the claim upon man's life is not in the realm of metaphysical speculation, but is, instead, a practical claim that is made upon man's will by absolute reality. The claim made upon a man's life must be answered by a commitment of one's whole being to God and by a life that embodies the truth of the absolute claim in practical living.[56] Since a man cannot really be a Christian all by himself but only in his togetherness with his fellow man; it follows that all genuine religious knowledge will beget practical and regulative living. A dichotomy cannot be made between worship and service. "We must at the same time remind ourselves that our worship of God is part of his service and our service of his worship."[57]

III. THE CHALLENGE OF REVELATION

In this section an attempt will be made to deal with what Baillie has stated was his "more personal" and "less abstract" point of view regarding revelation. He believes that every man is confronted in a realistic way by the challenge of revelation. This challenge of the divine upon the human life, according to him, is summed up in the biblical words "listen" and "obey." Man is to "listen to the indicative and obey the imperative."[58] The challenge of God's revelation, then, visits everyone as a very personal and practical affair.

<u>Attend to the divine claim.</u> The question that is often raised regarding God's revelation is why does God not declare himself more plainly? Baillie states that this question is raised by those who are often seeking a sign or "fool-proof" evidence for God's existence. But he asks in return: "What sign would we accept?"[59] In Baillie's opinion, God has done all he can for man's enlightenment and salvation in Jesus Christ without destroying man's freedom of inquiry.[60] The problem, he believes, lies not with God's revelation but with man's response. If man says that he is not aware of any self-disclosure by God, then Baillie believes that man needs to be asked if he is genuinely listening to God. Man cannot expect to receive more enlightenment from God if he has not responded to the revelation he has already received. God's revelation comes to man through many media. But revelation always comes in the form of a demand. It is a divine claim that is made upon a person's life.[61]

The knowledge of God comes to man in the human situation of life where he is inseparably bound up with his fellow man.[62] God's claim upon a man's life may be felt in the recurrent doubt about some habitual practice whose honesty is in question; it may be experienced in an uncomfortable feeling about some indulgence or prejudices that are harbored in one's life. Man's search for God may involve a search for the thing that hinders his response to the divine claim. Man must attend to the revelation he has already received before more illumination will be granted.[63]

There are many in our day who profess complete uncertainty about the deep things of God. They complain that God has not revealed Himself to them in a sufficiently convincing way. But perhaps this complaint is no better grounded than the former complaint about lack of opportunities for service. What if it is not God who fails to speak but we who fail to listen as we ought? Was not that what Jesus meant when He said, "If they hear not Moses and the prophets, neither will they be persuaded, though one rose from the dead?"[64]

Absolute obligation. Baillie has contended throughout his theology that the Christian faith is essentially trust. Trust is man's complete reliance on God and the commitment of himself fully to God's guardianship.[65] If man has heard the divine claim, then he must respond by obedience to that claim. Man cannot expect more light from God until he responds to the light he has already received. Man has received enough illumination about God through Jesus Christ to know what he has to do in life. If one yields his life in trust to the ultimate, although he may "see through a mirror dimly" now, he is assured that in the revelation in Christ there is all he needs to know about his ultimate concern.[66]

According to Baillie, the divine claim that is made upon man's life is absolute. The unconditional or absolute demand that confronts man in his consciousness of value contains in itself the recognition of the holy God who is its source. "No obligation can be absolute which does not derive from the Absolute."[67] It is also affirmed that there can be no moral obligation to an absolute if the absolute is not apprehended as personal. The challenge of revelation confronts man with an absolute obligation which comes from the personal God of the universe.[68]

The claim of God upon man's life does not come in the abstract or in a vacuum. It comes in the midst of the human situation where other claims of life are made upon man. Man responds to this claim not in abstraction but in the midst of living. Therefore, Baillie believes that God's claim upon a man's life is very practical and personal. He stresses the primacy of practical reason. The source of the absolute obligation is the Absolute. Baillie's contention is that man's life is personally challenged in divine revelation by a living God who is actively present in the world. Religious knowledge is never, then, merely theoretical and speculative, but it is always practical and regulative. God's claim upon a man's life is not abstract but concrete in its demand of absolute commitment to the ultimate reality.

CHAPTER VI

SUMMARY AND CONCLUSIONS

The examination of Baillie's concept of religious knowledge, as undertaken in this study, has involved a continuous evaluation of his theology throughout and has, therefore, eliminated the necessity for extensive concluding analysis. Nevertheless, a few observations on Baillie's view of epistemology seem appropriate in order to draw together the findings of this inquiry.

I. A SUMMARY OF BAILLIE'S CONCEPT OF RELIGIOUS KNOWLEDGE

Baillie's whole theology is predicated on the reality of man's personal encounter with God. He makes no attempt to prove that knowledge is possible. He begins with the presupposition that man is a knowing subject. He believes that knowledge implies certitude, but he does not believe that the certitude of knowledge excludes the possibility of the knowledge of probabilities. A distinction is made by him between real knowledge and putative knowledge. This differentiation, in his opinion, allows truth to be realized. This is the difference in one knowing that he knows or does not know and merely thinking or opining that he knows or does not know. Although Baillie believes that man's knowledge will always suffer certain limitations because man is finite, he does not believe that man's finitude will prohibit him from having any certitude in his knowledge. Man may have authentic contact with ultimate reality and absolute truth, but his theological formulations of this reality are always subject to correction, revision, and development. The distinction which Baillie makes between two kinds of knowledge, the knowledge of truth and the knowledge of reality, is his attempt to differentiate the primary and secondary elements in knowledge. He maintains that a distinction must be made between the authentic reality itself and the description about the reality. He argues that inferential knowledge is not satisfactory when direct knowledge is possible. The element of direct acquaintance is primary, and the discursive element is secondary in knowledge.

According to Baillie, religious knowledge is possible because man is able to commune directly with God. He believes that man is more directly confronted by the reality of God than any other reality. Man's acquaintance with God arises through a "non-sensuous perception" and is not limited to veridical knowledge.

The nature of revelation is interpreted by Baillie as a bifocal aspect of experience. From the human side man is led to a discovery of divine truth through the function of moral consciousness. The divine aspect of revelation is conceived as essentially the self-disclosure of God to man. While this process may be depicted as bifocal, Baillie insists that the initiative in revelation is always with God and not man. Baillie prefers the terms general and special revelation to the traditional terms, natural and revealed. But he still does not find this distinction completely satisfactory, because he believes that there is something special in all of God's revelation.

In Baillie's opinion, there is a universality of religious knowledge among all men at all times. Wherever there is genuine religious insight, its ultimate source is God. It is evident in much of Baillie's theology that Kant has greatly influenced him. This influence is apparent in Baillie's insistence that man's moral values provide a category of religious awareness through which God is revealed. The imago dei is the moral consciousness within man which provides the focal point for divine revelation. The imago dei in man's nature has been "spoiled" or "defaced" but not obliterated. It is, then, the point of contact in human nature for the reception of God's revelation.

Baillie's understanding of the epistemological status of natural religion follows the Kantian view of knowledge which limits scientific knowledge to the phenomenal world and which makes natural science incompetent to formulate a basis for belief in God. Nature, even in its mechanical uniformity, cannot be considered as a self-explanatory system. Nature, in itself, can only "half reveal" and "half conceal" God. The eye of faith is needed in order to discern the revelatory aspect of nature. Nature is impersonal in itself, but God is personal, and his revelation is manifested in personal communion.

Baillie makes no allowance for a complete discontinuity between nature and grace. He affirms that there must be a continuity between the natural life and the spiritual, otherwise man could not respond to God's revelation. No man is wholly outside of fellowship with God. Baillie prefers a scale of forms or degrees rather than a distinct point below which one could say that grace does not extend. In Baillie's opinion, man may deny God consciously, "with the top of his mind," but still believe in him unconsciously, "in the bottom of his heart." Intellectual denial of God's existence need not completely destroy one's spiritual life. Since Baillie argues that man is never completely out of a state of grace, he rejects any call for a single decisive experience of conversion.

Human discovery and divine revelation, Baillie believes, are complementary sides of the self-same fact of experience. Divine truth cannot be divided into a two source theory which would make revelation and reason alternatives appropriate to different areas. Revelation and reason are the divine and human sides in man's knowledge of God. This does not mean, however, that a distinction should not be made between revelation and discovery. Although none of man's knowledge is totally unrelated to God's self-disclosure, man's religious knowledge is of a different degree from the rest of his knowledge. A discovery is made by someone, but a disclosure is made by one to another. No true knowledge of God can be explained by beginning from the human side. All true knowledge is determined by the object and not the subject.

Revelation is always given within a personal relationship. Baillie believes that this is not only true concerning the way of knowing, but it is also true concerning the content of knowledge. Revelation is not only a disclosure from subject to subject, but it is a disclosure of subject to subject. Revelation is not information about God but the self-revelation of God. Baillie's central theme throughout his writings is that God is known by man not by argument but by being directly confronted by the divine presence. Knowledge of God's existence is not the result of an inference of any kind; it comes only through direct personal encounter with God. The true office of argument, as Baillie understands it, is to lead men back to the point where they can again become self-conscious of the direct presence of God which has never really left them.

History is the medium through which God's revelation comes to man. God's presence does not come to man in a vacuum, but always comes in conjunction with man's knowledge of others and the corporeal world. History has meaning only if it has a center. Christ is the center of history. History, however, is not revelatory as such. The events in history are conditioned by the human experience. History is always "events plus meaning." The consummation of God's revelation in history is realized in the Incarnation. In Jesus Christ the interaction of the divine and human are discernible in the one who was "both God and man." The fullness of God's revelation in history is centered in Christ. He becomes the pivotal point that gives history its meaning.

Although man's encounter with God brings him into an immediacy with God, this encounter is a "mediated immediacy." God's encounter with man does not take place in a vacuum. It is an experience that occurs in and through familiar human experience. God's presence is mediated to man through various media, but supremely through the Incarnation.

A direct awareness of God's presence is realized by faith. Man has a "sense of the presence of God" which is an awareness of the claim made upon man from beyond himself. The "sense of the presence of God" is a perceptional mode which is beyond the ordinary sense of perception. Faith is, then, a mode of apprehension of the divine and a mode of active response to that apprehension. Therefore, there can be no apprehension without commitment and no commitment without apprehension. For Baillie, faith is not based on religious experience, because faith, if it is authentic, is not deduced from religious experience but is a constitutive part of it.

Baillie has given the role of intuition a significant place in his concept of religious knowledge. In his view of intuition, he has disassociated himself from the view that intuition is an apprehension of a truth or a proposition. He places the emphasis on direct insight and immediacy rather than the discursive element in knowledge. His contention is that the element of commitment takes precedence over assent to propositional truths about God. He acknowledges that trust in God is based on grounds for this trust; yet he declares that it is difficult to articulate in verbal form what these grounds are. Commitment always takes precedence over assent.

Baillie's understanding of the role of language in religious knowledge is predicated upon his view of the personal nature of revelation. The purpose of the Bible is realized in the role it bears as the medium which contains the written record of <u>Heilsgeschichte.</u> The Bible is the written witness to the intercourse of event and interpretation. Baillie has rejected a dictation theory of inspiration and has also acknowledged the fallibility of the human aspect of the Bible, but, nevertheless, he believes in "verbal inspiration," if it is not regarded as plenary. The written word cannot be equated with the revelation itself, however, for its purpose is to serve as a medium of revelation.

Logical positivists have insisted that no knowledge can be accepted as true unless it is capable of verification in terms of sense experience. Baillie has contended that no one can arbitrarily set up a principle and demand that all areas of experience are verifiable by it alone. He asserts that the verification of man's ethical, aesthetic, and religious knowledge should be administered not by a return to corporeal reality, but by returning to the area of experience out of which each emerged.

The criterion of revelation is determined by faith's primary apprehension of the divine. Religion can be tested only from within and not by standards established apart from revelation. Since Christ is the fullness of revelation, revelation is judged by his disclosure.

According to one of Baillie's basic premises, religious knowledge finds its real meaning in practical application. Religious knowledge and morality cannot be separated. The roots of religion are in man's consciousness of value; but the source of the moral obligation is the living God himself. Religion differs from morality in that it always has a transcendental reference. The Gospel of Jesus has provided a way of life for his followers. In the Christ-event, the "reign of God" has been inaugurated. The New Testament describes this way in terms of agapé and koinōnia.

The Christian's hope for everlasting life is based on his personal knowledge of the eternal God. This hope is rooted in man's daily communion with the eternal God. If man is able to commune with God, which Baillie believes he can, then man matters to God; and if he matters to God, he will share eternity with God.

Man's religious knowledge is not something regulated to the abstract dimension. Revelation presents itself to man as a challenge to "listen" and "obey." Having heard the indicative of the divine revelation, man is to obey God's imperative. The revelation of God presents itself to man in a very personal manner and requires absolute obedience of the one addressed.

II. POSITIVE VALUES IN BAILLIE'S CONCEPT OF RELIGIOUS KNOWLEDGE

There are many positive values which could be noted in Baillie's concept of religious knowledge. A brief examination will be made of a few of these positive contributions.

The <u>personal element in revelation.</u> Central to Baillie's concept of epistemology is his view of the personal nature of religious knowledge. In the personal aspect of religious knowledge, the nature of revelation itself is correlated with the content of the disclosure. In some traditions, God has been acknowledged as the subject of the nature of revelation but not as the content of the revelation. In Baillie's view, the content of revelation is God himself.

If God is the revealer, what he discloses to man is his divine presence. The revelation of God in personal encounter affirms the directness and immediacy of the divine relationship with man. Inferential knowledge acquired indirectly cannot contain the certitude as that which is contained in direct personal experience. Man is confronted not by an object of theoretical knowledge but with an absolute obligation.

<u>Inferential knowledge and revelation</u>. Since the chief emphasis in Baillie's concept of the reception of revelation is his insistence on the direct encounter of man with God, it logically follows that God is not known inferentially. If God could be known by inference from any area, this would place the initiative for religious knowledge with man. Baillie believes that the only true religious argument for the being of God comes in actual, personal communion with the divine. When the personal nature of revelation has been correctly understood, the weaknesses of subjectivism and objectivism are avoided. Subjectivism becomes a problem when the initiative in revelation is said to arise from within man himself. Objectivism becomes problematic when one attempts to equate the "word of God" with facts or propositions. Baillie's position eludes both of these problems. According to him, the initiative in revelation comes from without man as God confronts him directly; and God is known as the divine subject who is not an object that can be controlled by man. Revelation is not based on inferential knowledge of any kind. God's revelation is not given in propositional truths but through his self-communication. The truth, therefore, is not a truth about God's disclosure but the self-communication itself. What God bestows in revelation is communion, not information.

<u>The universality of religious knowledge</u>. Baillie asserts that all men have been made aware of God's presence to some degree, and none have ever been completely devoid of his revelation. He bases his belief in this principle on the premise that the <u>imago dei</u> has not been obliterated in man and, therefore, serves as the point of contact in all men for the self-revelation of the divine. It is evident to Baillie that any concept of the total obliteration of the <u>imago dei</u> is unrealistic. All men are able to have an awareness of God because all men have a point of contact with the divine. Baillie's view seems valid. If God has to create the <u>imago dei</u> anew, then man would be no higher than the nonrational animals below him. If man is absorbed into the humanity of God as projected in Jesus as the "real man," then man is not a responsible self and his freedom and real significance are annihilated. Revelation is made to a rational being who has received the capacity to respond in the creative process. The fact that this capacity within man has not been completely obliterated or completely absorbed is evident in the awareness of the presence of God to some degree in men today.

<u>Revelation and human discovery</u>. Revelation, as Baillie presents it, is a bifocal process. Human discovery and divine revelation are complementary sides of the self-same fact of experience. He does not mean by this, however, that they are two aspects of the same process in the sense that all truth is both discovered and revealed. Man's rational

faculty enables him to discover all he can from the natural world or other media, but this inferred knowledge will not of necessity lead to absolute truth. Man may discover many things in the areas of science, medicine, and education and still be oblivious to the reality of God from whom all knowledge ultimately comes. If man were able to arrive at a knowledge of God by his own discovery, then the initiative in religious knowledge would be with man instead of God. Revelation cannot be equated with human discovery.

Mediated immediacy. Man's knowledge of God is direct and personal; but this does not imply, in Baillie's opinion, that God is ever present to man apart from all other presences. God's presence confronts man in a "mediated immediacy." Baillie's view affirms the necessity of history and the Church in man's religious knowledge. Man does not encounter God in isolation but within the human situation.

God's revelation comes to individuals only within the fellowship of faith. God is mediated supremely to man within history in the Incarnation. Here the Incarnate one becomes the mediator who directs sinful man to a gracious God. If God could be known in unveiled immediacy, then his mystery and holiness would be totally dissolved. Baillie's concept of "mediated immediacy" preserves the necessary concept of God's holiness.

Nature as a medium of revelation. It is Baillie's contention that man cannot arrive at a knowledge of God by speculative means based on a consideration of the natural world apart from the personal self-disclosure of God. He believes that the natural realm in itself is not revelatory but may become a medium of revelation. General revelation is not able within itself to terminate in special revelation. The natural realm is impersonal, and man cannot deduce from this medium the personal nature of God. It is not simply a question of epistemology but of ontology. God is not present as personal redemptive love in the natural order. The problem of evil precludes this possibility. Nature may serve as a medium of revelation only to those who are already aware of God's presence within their hearts.

The Scriptures as a medium of revelation. According to Baillie, the unique nature of the Bible as revelatory is understood in the role it bears as the medium which contains the written witness to God's redemptive activity. The Bible is a medium to mediate the immediacy of the living God. It's purpose is not to serve as a manual of doctrinal information but to bear witness to the personal God who is seeking to reveal himself. The Bible is considered authoritative for the Christian not because it is inerrant in a plenary sense; but because it is the unique prophetic and apostolic witness to God's revelation. The authority of the Bible, however, does not reside in an impersonal book, but it is based on authority of the holy God who is mediated to men through the written witness.

<u>The verification of religious knowledge</u>. Baillie has sought to demonstrate that verification of religious knowledge cannot be limited to sense experience, as logical empiricists claim. He believes that religious knowledge should be verified on its own level. Theological judgments are verifiable by reference only to faith's primary apprehension of the divine. The logical positivists have asserted that "no statement of fact is meaningful unless it can be verified in sense experience." But this principle cannot be verified by the only two types of statements the positivists believe are true: the strictly logical and those established by sense experience. Neither of these two types can verify the verification principle itself. Baillie's insistence that statements be verified by returning to the area of experience out of which they emerged is more realistic than the one advocated by the positivists. Religion can be tested only from within. If the Christian revelation is tested by some standard apart from the revelation itself, the standard becomes the ultimate ground and is subject itself to no rational test. A claim to revelation is tested by its ability to fulfill its own premises. Since Christ is the unique revelation of God, he becomes the criterion for judging the truth or falsification to any claim to revelation.

<u>Religious knowledge and morality</u>. All meaningful religious knowledge, Baillie attests, must culminate in action. Religion and morality are bound in an inseparable union. Man is able to encounter God personally; but man must realize his solidaristic involvement with humanity. Authentic religious knowledge will issue in service. A Christian's service toward others in society is not a separate action toward God, but is the only genuine way man serves God. Man's encounter with God always brings with it an absolute obligation. Although Baillie has been accused of identifying religion and morality, he avoids this fallacy by stressing a transcendental reference. The moral challenge that man encounters in his consciousness of value is not distinct from God; it is the impact of the personal God himself who is challenging man. Man is obedient to this claim as he gives his life in unselfish service toward his fellow man. In this view Baillie has correlated the theoretical with the practical, and the abstract with the concrete.

III. OBJECTIONS TO BAILLIE'S CONCEPT OF RELIGIOUS KNOWLEDGE

While Baillie's theory of religious knowledge has many positive points, several criticisms may be made. These criticisms will be expounded below.

The inadequacy of unconscious faith. In his understanding of the universality of religious knowledge, Baillie maintains that man may deny God with the "top of his mind" and still believe in him in the "bottom of his heart." He believes that faith must be conscious, but that it does not necessarily have to be conscious of itself. But this denial of genuine conscious faith certainly is inadequate for man's spiritual life. This view is not in accord with Baillie's major thesis of revelation by personal encounter. If man has been confronted by God, he may not realize all that is involved in this encounter, but surely he must be conscious of the confrontation itself for it to have significance for him. Genuine faith can exist only where there is conscious commitment. Man's volition must be allowed. God encounters man on the conscious level; and man responds or rejects God's presence on the conscious level. Faith can be genuine only on the conscious level because it is on this level that commitment is made.

Conversion and commitment. Strictures must also be directed against Baillie's concept of conversion. Baillie has severely criticized Christian groups that call for a crisis experience of conversion. According to him, an infant may be baptized while someone else makes a commitment for him. When he reaches maturity he seals the commitment that was made for him while he was a child. This view, however, violates Baillie's principle concerning the necessity of personal commitment in religious knowledge. If God's revelation presents itself to man in the form of an absolute obligation, can someone else make a genuine commitment for the one to whom it comes? In experiential religion each man must make his own commitment to God as he is confronted by his divine presence. Commitment to God must be free, conscious, and voluntary. If confrontation with God is personal and from subject to subject, commitment is made on a personal basis and not by proxy.

The inspiration of the Scriptures. A view which Baillie expounds that is totally inconsistent with the rest of his concept of religious knowledge is his belief in "verbal inspiration." Exactly what Baillie means by the phrase verbal inspiration is not certain. Since he has rejected plenary inspiration, he does not need to verify how every word of the Bible is inspired; but he does need to demonstrate how certain words and ideas can be inspired verbally without resulting in propositional revelation. Baillie's whole epistemological system has been directed against the idea of inferential knowledge, and it is illogical for him to propose a view that undermines his own basic premise. He has acknowledged that the vehicle conveying the record of revelation need not be infallible. He has also declared that the basic purpose of the Bible is to bear witness to the redemptive activity of God. Baillie's view of verbal inspiration, therefore, does not complement his theory of religious knowledge but impairs it.

The symbolic nature of language. Baillie is unwilling to affirm that all theological statements are symbolical. When one avers that God is personal, Baillie is convinced that this is an intelligible assertion that does not point beyond itself. But can man speak of the Infinite and one's experience with him in any way other than in symbolic language? Even the term person as applied to God is symbolic and not literally true. Personality is the highest reality of which man is aware, but God cannot be described as a person beside others. It may be said that God is "personal" but he is not "a" person. Personality may be the highest form of reality about which man is aware, but it still might not be the highest form of reality there is. This in no way prevents man from referring to God as "Thou." But it does cause one to be aware that God may be more than "Thou" but surely not less. Man can only depict ultimate reality in changing symbolic categories. Man bears witness to his religious confrontation, but his interpretation of this experience can never be equated or finalized with the articulation of the inner experience.

The Incarnation and revelation. In Baillie's view of the Incarnation, a certain ambiguity is evident. Although he declares that the Incarnation is the essence of the Christian faith, he is reluctant to affirm that God is uniquely Incarnate in Jesus. He believes that God's spirit has been manifested through many men. In his later writings, Baillie seems to have modified his position somewhat and emphasizes the "uniqueness and irreplaceableness of God's self-revelation" in Jesus Christ. Nevertheless, Baillie needs to emphasize with greater clarity a belief which is central to the Christian faith. If God has disclosed himself "fully" in Jesus the Christ, then, this is indisputably a unique event in human history.

CONCLUSION

Except for the objections noted above, Baillie's view of religious knowledge seems logical and coherent. His basic premise of revelation as personal is pursued throughout the ramifications of his theory of religious knowledge. It is evident in his concepts of general and special revelation, in his understanding of the nature and verification of religious assertions, and in the relationship of religious knowledge and morality. God's disclosure to man is always personal, and man's response to this revelation is likewise personal. In the Incarnation of the Logos, God's revelation has become uniquely personal and historical.

NOTES

PREFACE
1. Wolfhart Pannenberg, Jesus - God and Man, p. 131.
2. John Baillie, "Confessions of a Transplanted Scot," Contemporary American Theology: Theological Autobiographies, p. 52.
3. Ibid.

CHAPTER ONE
1. David Elton Trueblood, Philosophy of Religion, p. 55.
2. David Elton Trueblood, General Philosophy, pp. 25-29. Cf. Trueblood, Philosophy of Religion, pp. 54-56.
3. Trueblood, Philosophy of Religion, p. 57.
4. Ibid.
5. Along with this presupposition, the writer also accepts the following general presuppositions of knowledge as set forth by Georgia Harkness in Foundations of Christian Knowledge, pp. 42-50, 92-93. a. The primary criterion of truth is the coherence of all available evidence. b. The discovery of knowledge is a function of our total experience, not of intellectual processes alone. c. All knowledge except of formal relation is incomplete, yet much is dependable. d. Truth is objective and stable, though our apprehension of it is subjective, partial, and variable. e. The human mind and the external world are organic to each other. f. For any knowledge, certain presuppositions are necessary: the existence and dependability of the external world, a common world of experience, the trustworthiness of our mental powers, and the interpretative activity of the mind. g. Values are facts.
6. A. N. Whitehead, Adventures of Ideas, pp. 232-233.
7. John Baillie, The Sense of the Presence of God, pp. 1-2. Cf. John Baillie, The Interpretation of Religion: An Introductory Study of Theological Principles, pp. 373-374.
8. Baillie, The Sense of the Presence of God, p. 2.
9. Ibid.
10. Ibid., p. 3.
11. Ibid., p. 5.
12. Ibid., pp. 5-7.
13. Ibid., p. 8.
14. Ibid., pp. 9-12. Cf. Baillie, The Interpretation of Religion, pp. 373-380.
15. Baillie, The Sense of the Presence of God, p. 12.
16. Ibid., pp. 15-17.
17. Ibid., pp. 19-20.
18. Ibid., pp. 32-33.

NOTES

19. Ibid., p. 33.
20. Ibid., pp. 33-36, 88.
21. Ibid., p. 17.
22. John Baillie, Our Knowledge of God, pp. 204-208. Cf. Baillie, The Sense of the Presence of God, pp. 34-36.
23. Baillie, Our Knowledge of God, pp. 208-211.
24. Ibid., p. 212.
25. Ibid.
26. Ibid., pp. 212-213.
27. Baillie, The Sense of the Presence of God, p. 18.
28. Baillie, Our Knowledge of God, pp. 155-157.
29. Ibid., p. 148.
30. Ibid., p. 166.
31. Rufus M. Jones, The New Quest, p. 146.
32. Baillie, The Sense of the Presence of God, p. 63. Cf. Alfred Jules Ayer, Language, Truth, and Logic, p. 71.
33. Baillie, The Sense of the Presence of God, p. 27.
34. Baillie, Our Knowledge of God, p. 217. See Chapter IV for a further discussion of this aspect of Baillie's thought.
35. Baillie, The Sense of the Presence of God, p. 52.
36. Ibid., pp. 52-54. C. B. Martin has attempted to reduce Baillie's concept of personal encounter with God to the level of personal feelings and sensations. He has also noted that no tests were allowed by Baillie to distinguish genuine from ungenuine religious experience. See Antony Flew and Alasdair MacIntyre, editors, New Essays in Philosophical Theology, pp. 76-95. Martin's position, however, does not seem valid. In The Sense of the Presence of God, which was published after Martin's article was written, Baillie has set forth his view of the perceptive and cognitive aspect of faith; and he has also noted the criterion that he believes is justified in "testing" religious knowledge. This is discussed more thoroughly in Chapter IV.
37. Baillie, The Sense of the Presence of God, pp. 52-54.
38. Ibid., pp. 52-55, 89-91, 259-261.
39. John Baillie, The Idea of Revelation in Recent Thought, p. 19.
40. Ibid., pp. 22-26.
41. Baillie, The Interpretation of Religion, p. 10.
42. Baillie, The Sense of the Presence of God, pp. 187-188.
43. Baillie, The Interpretation of Religion, pp. 458-466. Cf. Baillie, The Idea of Revelation in Recent Thought, pp. 19-27. For a discussion of the relationship of revelation and reason see L. Harold DeWolf, A Theology of the Living Church, pp. 33-45 and Leonard Hodgson, For Faith and Freedom, I, 80-90.

NOTES

CHAPTER TWO
1. Georgia Harkness, Foundations of Christian Knowledge, p. 73.
2. John Baillie, Our Knowledge of God, pp. 42-43.
3. John Baillie, The Sense of the Presence of God, p. 188. Cf. John Baillie, The Idea of Revelation in Recent Thought, pp. 132-133.
4. Baillie, The Sense of the Presence of God, p. 188.
5. Ibid.
6. Ibid., p. 186.
7. Baillie, The Idea of Revelation in Recent Thought, p. 43.
8. Ibid., p. 129.
9. Baillie, The Sense of the Presence of God, p. 188. Cf. Baillie, The Idea of Revelation in Recent Thought, pp. 43, 125-133; John Baillie, Invitation to Pilgrimage, pp. 144-145.
10. John Baillie, The Roots of Religion in the Human Soul, pp. 74-75. Cf. John Baillie, The Interpretation of Religion, pp. 64-65.
11. Baillie, The Roots of Religion in the Human Soul, p. 74.
12. Baillie, The Interpretation of Religion, p. 64.
13. Baillie, Our Knowledge of God, p. 35.
14. Baillie, The Sense of the Presence of God, p. 187.
15. Ibid.
16. Ibid., p. 188.
17. Ibid., pp. 187-188.
18. Baillie, Our Knowledge of God, pp. 6, 17-43.
19. Ibid., p. 6.
20. Ibid., pp. 6-7. Cf. Baillie, The Sense of the Presence of God, pp. 186-188.
21. Baillie, Invitation to Pilgrimage, p. 100.
22. Baillie, The Idea of Revelation in Recent Thought, pp. 19-27.
23. Baillie, Invitation to Pilgrimage, pp. 100-101.
24. Baillie, The Sense of the Presence of God, pp. 187-188.
25. Baillie, The Interpretation of Religion, pp. 257, 460-461.
26. Ibid., pp. 117, 257, 390, 461-462.
27. John Baillie, "The Logic of Religion," p. 11. Cf. also John Baillie, "Happiness Once More," p. 82; Baillie, The Sense of the Presence of God, pp. 18, 88, 256.
28. Baillie, Our Knowledge of God, p. 162. Cf. Baillie, The Interpretation of Religion, pp. 462-464.
29. John Baillie, "The Subliminal Consciousness as an Aid to the Interpretation of Religious Experience," p. 355.
30. Baillie, Our Knowledge of God, pp. 17-19.
31. See Karl Barth, The Epistle to the Romans; The Word of God and the Word of Man. Modifications in Barth's position are evident in

NOTES

A Shorter Commentary on Romans and *The Humanity of God*.
    32. John Baillie, "Confessions of a Transplanted Scot," p. 52.
    33. John Baillie and Hugh Martin, editors, *Revelation*, p. 48.
    34. *Ibid.*, p. 53.
    35. Karl Barth, *The Epistle to the Romans*, p. 29.
    36. *Ibid.*
    37. Karl Barth, *Church Dogmatics*, I, 1, p. 442.
    38. *Ibid.*, p. 448.
    39. Baillie, *Our Knowledge of God*, p. 22.
    40. *Ibid.*, p. 23.
    41. *Ibid.*, p. 24.
    42. *Ibid.*, p. 27. Cf. Baillie, *Invitation to Pilgrimage*, pp. 17-18.
    43. Baillie, *The Interpretation of Religion*, p. 464.
    44. John Baillie, *A Reasoned Faith*, pp. 96-97. Cf. John Baillie, *A Diary of Private Prayer*, p. 19.
    45. Baillie, *The Interpretation of Religion*, p. 162.
    46. Baillie, *Our Knowledge of God*, p. 24. Cf. Baillie, *Invitation to Pilgrimage*, pp. 100-101.
    47. Karl Barth, *Church Dogmatics*, III, 1, pp. ix-x.
    48. Barth, *Church Dogmatics*, I, 1, p. 272; II, 1, pp. 147-149; IV, 1, p. 576; IV, 2, p. 560.
    49. Barth, *Church Dogmatics*, I, 1, p. 273; II, 2, pp. 560, 566.
    50. Barth, *Church Dogmatics*, III, 2, p. 324; IV, 1, pp. 480-484; III, 2, pp. 265, 267, 277.
    51. Barth, *Church Dogmatics*, III, 1, pp. 270-273.
    52. David L. Mueller, "The Theology of Karl Barth and the Nineteenth Century," *Religion and Life*, (Winter, 1964-65), p. 89.
    53. Barth, *Church Dogmatics*, II, 1, pp. 284-286.
    54. Barth, *Church Dogmatics*, IV, 1, pp. 317, 348, 353, 391; IV, 2, p. 49; I, 2, pp. 163-164.
    55. Barth, *Church Dogmatics*, IV, 2, pp. 47-48; III, 2, p. 86.
    56. Emil Brunner, *Revelation and Reason: The Christian Doctrine of Faith and Knowledge*, pp. 58-79.
    57. Baillie, *Our Knowledge of God*, p. 32.
    58. *Ibid.*, pp. 31-33.
    59. See Albert C. Knudson, *The Religious Teaching of the Old Testament*, p. 235; H. H. Rowley, *The Faith of Israel: Aspects of Old Testament Thought*, pp. 74-89.
    60. Genesis 1:26f; 5:1.
    61. Genesis 2:7.
    62. *Ibid.*, Cf. Rowley, *op. cit.*, p. 85.
    63. S. R. Driver, *The Book of Genesis*, p. 15.

NOTES

64. Gerhard von Rad, Old Testament Theology, I, 147. Rad states: "Thus, through the image of God in man Creation, in addition to coming from God, receives a particular ordering towards God." Knudson declares: "We must, then, find the image of God in man's participation in the higher personal or spiritual life of God." Knudson, op. cit., p. 235. H. Wheeler Robinson says: "Whatever the doubtful phrase, 'the image of God,' may mean, it is certainly intended to recognize man's unique relation to God, and his supremacy over the animal world." H. Wheeler Robinson, Religious Ideas of the Old Testament, p. 85. See also Rowley, op. cit., pp. 79-98; Millar Burrows, An Outline Of Biblical Theology, pp. 141-145; Frank E. Eakin, Jr., The Religion and Culture of Israel, pp. 116-118; Walter Eichrodt, Man In the Old Testament, p. 30f.; Ludwig Koehler, Old Testament Theology, pp. 146-148; E. C. Rust, Nature and Man in Biblical Thought, p. 121f.; Frank Stagg, Polarities of Man's Existence in Biblical Perspective, pp. 19-44.

65. Rad, loc. cit.

66. See Genesis 9:6; Psalm 8:5; Esekiel 28:12; Ephesians 4:24; Colossians 3:10; James 3:9.

67. Baillie, Our Knowledge of God, p. 38.

68. Ibid., p. 43.

69. Ibid., p. 41.

70. Ibid., pp. 42-43.

71. Baillie, The Sense of the Presence of God, pp. 187-188.

72. Ibid., p. 188.

73. Baillie, The Idea of Revelation in Recent Thought, pp. 125-133. Cf. Baillie, Our Knowledge of God, pp. 40-41.

74. John Baillie, "The Present Situation in Theology," pp. 5-6.

75. Baillie, The Interpretation of Religion, pp. 84-85.

76. Baillie, The Idea of Revelation in Recent Thought, p. 70. See William Temple, Nature, Man and God, p. 306.

77. Temple, Nature, Man and God, p. 306.

78. Baillie, The Idea of Revelation in Recent Thought, p. 72.

79. Baillie, The Interpretation of Religion, p. 86. Cf. Baillie, "The Present Situation in Theology," p. 12.

80. Baillie, The Idea of Revelation in Recent Thought, p. 74.

81. Baillie, "The Present Situation in Theology," p. 19.

82. Baillie, The Idea of Revelation in Recent Thought, p. 74.

83. Ibid., p. 78.

84. Ibid., p. 80.

85. Ibid.

86. Clifford Braman, "The Philosophical Theology of John Baillie," (Unpublished doctor's dissertation, New York University, New York,

NOTES

1954), p. 66.
87. Baillie, Our Knowledge of God, p. 178.
88. Ibid., p. 96.
89. Ibid., p. 94.
90. Ibid., p. 102.
91. Baillie, The Interpretation of Religion, p. 448.
92. Ibid., p. 458. Cf. John Baillie, The Place of Jesus Christ in Modern Christianity, pp. 104-105.
93. Baillie, A Reasoned Faith, p. 98.
94. Baillie, The Interpretation of Religion, p. 458. Leonard Hodgson understands the Christian revelation as a part of general revelation. See Leonard Hodgson, For Faith and Freedom, II, 3-4. It is not likely that Baillie would agree with this statement.
95. Baillie, The Interpretation of Religion, pp. 458-459. Cf. Baillie, The Idea of Revelation in Recent Thought, pp. 19-20.
96. Nels F. S. Ferré, The Christian Understanding of God, p. 160.

CHAPTER THREE
1. John Baillie, The Sense of the Presence of God, p. 188.
2. John Baillie, The Idea of Revelation in Recent Thought, pp. 19-20.
3. Ibid., p. 24.
4. Ibid., pp. 25-27.
5. John Baillie, Our Knowledge of God, p. 166.
6. Ibid., p. 108. Cf. Plato, Laws, Book 10, pp. 296-387.
7. Baillie, Our Knowledge of God, pp. 107-108.
8. Ibid., p. 111.
9. Etienne Gilson, Reason and Revelation in the Middle Ages, pp. 81-84.
10. Baillie, Our Knowledge of God, pp. 112-113.
11. Ibid., p. 115.
12. Ibid., pp. 122-123.
13. Ibid., p. 124.
14. Ibid., p. 126.
15. Ibid., p. 132.
16. John Baillie, "Confessions of a Transplanted Scot," p. 52.
17. John A. Mackay, "John Baillie, A Lyrical Tribute and Appraisal," Scottish Journal of Theology, (September, 1956), p. 231.
18. John Baillie, "The Fundamental Task of the Theological Seminary," pp. 266-267.
19. Baillie, Our Knowledge of God, p. 143.
20. Ibid., p. 240.
21. Ibid.

NOTES

22. Ibid.
23. Ibid., p. 244.
24. Ibid., pp. 244-245.
25. Ibid., p. 245.
26. John Baillie, "The Logic of Religion," p. 6.
27. Baillie, "Confessions of a Transplanted Scot," p. 50.
28. Baillie, Our Knowledge of God, pp. 137-141, Cf. John Baillie, The Interpretation of Religion, pp. 359-360; John Baillie, The Roots of Religion in the Human Soul, pp. 110-112.
29. Baillie, Our Knowledge of God, p. 178.
30. Ibid., pp. 180-187.
31. Ibid., p. 180.
32. Ibid., pp. 185-186.
33. John Baillie, Invitation to Pilgrimage, p. 98.
34. Ibid., pp. 98-106. Cf. John Baillie, The Belief in Progress, pp. 65-74.
35. Baillie, The Belief in Progress, p. 66.
36. Baillie, The Idea of Revelation in Recent Thought, pp. 66-68.
37. Ibid., p. 70.
38. Ibid., p. 80.
39. Ibid.
40. Baillie, The Interpretation of Religion, p. 466.
41. 2 Corinthians 5:19.
42. John Baillie, A Reasoned Faith, p. 123.
43. Ibid., pp. 153-161.
44. Baillie, The Sense of the Presence of God, p. 204.
45. Baillie, A Reasoned Faith, p. 161. Cf. Baillie, Our Knowledge of God, p. 186-187.
46. John Baillie, The Place of Jesus Christ in Modern Christianity, p. 116.
47. Baillie, The Interpretation of Religion, p. 469.
48. Baillie, The Place of Jesus Christ in Modern Christianity, p. 118.
49. Baillie, The Interpretation of Religion, p. 469.
50. Baillie, The Place of Jesus Christ in Modern Christianity, p. 121.
51. Baillie, Our Knowledge of God, p. 180.
52. Baillie, The Sense of the Presence of God, pp. 209-211.
53. John Baillie, "World Mission of the Church: The Contemporary Scene," p. 168.
54. John Baillie, "The Given Word: The Message of the Unvarying Gospel," p. 456.
55. Ibid., pp. 458-459.
56. Baillie, The Idea of Revelation in Recent Thought, p. 80.

NOTES

57. John Baillie, "An Impression and Its Interpretation," p. 6.
58. Baillie, The Interpretation of Religion, p. 468.
59. Baillie, "An Impression and Its Interpretation," pp. 6-8. Cf. Baillie, The Interpretation of Religion, p. 468.
60. Baillie, The Roots of Religion in the Human Soul, p. 97.
61. Baillie, The Idea of Revelation in Recent Thought, p. 81.
62. Ibid. In Genesis 1:3, God speaks and it is done. "And God said, 'let there be light;' and there was light." Isaiah states: "So shall my word be that goes forth from my mouth; it shall not return to me empty, but it shall accomplish that which I purpose, and prosper in the thing for which I sent it." Isaiah 55:11.
63. Baillie, The Idea of Revelation in Recent Thought, p. 19.
64. Baillie, Our Knowledge of God, p. 191.
65. Baillie, The Idea of Revelation in Recent Thought, p. 60.
66. Ibid., p. 61. For a good discussion of mystery and revelation see Michael B. Foster, Mystery and Philosophy, and John Dillenberger, God Hidden and Revealed.
67. Baillie, The Idea of Revelation in Recent Thought, p. 64.
68. Ibid., pp. 65-66.
69. Baillie, Our Knowledge of God, p. 166.
70. See Baillie, The Interpretation of Religion, pp. 318-348; The Idea of Revelation in Recent Thought, pp. 19, 61; Our Knowledge of God, pp. 6, 8, 17, 126, 132, 148, 155, 166, 175, 197; The Sense of the Presence of God, pp. 20, 33, 54, 88, 204.
71. Baillie, Our Knowledge of God, p. 126.
72. Baillie, The Interpretation of Religion, p. 360.
73. Ibid., p. 392. Cf. Baillie, The Roots of Religion in the Human Soul, pp. 100, 111-112.
74. John Baillie, "Why I Believe in God," p. 4.
75. Baillie, The Sense of the Presence of God, pp. 60-61, 187-188.
76. Baillie, Our Knowledge of God, pp. 174-175.
77. Ibid., p. 178.
78. Ibid., p. 181. Cf. Baillie, The Sense of the Presence of God, p. 259.
79. Baillie, The Sense of the Presence of God, pp. 259-260.
80. See H. Wheeler Robinson, Redemption and Revelation, pp. 95-195, for a discussion of the principle of mediation.
81. Baillie, The Sense of the Presence of God, p. 260.
82. Ibid., p. 117. Cf. Baillie, Our Knowledge of God, p. 178.
83. Baillie, Our Knowledge of God, pp. 178-180.
84. Ibid., pp. 179-180.
85. Ibid., p. 180. Cf. Baillie, The Sense of the Presence of God,

NOTES

p. 260.
86. Baillie, Our Knowledge of God, p. 180.
87. Ibid., p. 220.
88. Ibid., pp. 221-222.
89. Baillie, The Sense of the Presence of God, p. 17.
90. Ibid., p. 18. Cf. Baillie, Our Knowledge of God, p. 222.
91. Baillie, Our Knowledge of God, p. 224.
92. Ibid., p. 227.
93. Baillie, The Idea of Revelation in Recent Thought, p. 24.
94. Baillie, The Sense of the Presence of God, pp. 17-18.
95. Baillie, The Idea of Revelation in Recent Thought, p. 49.
96. William Temple, Nature, Man and God, p. 322.
97. Ibid., p. 317.
98. Baillie, The Sense of the Presence of God, pp. 88-89.
99. Ibid., p. 90.
100. Ibid.
101. Ibid., pp. 90-92.
102. Baillie, The Interpretation of Religion, pp. 230-234.
103. Baillie, The Sense of the Presence of God, p. 65.
104. Ibid., pp. 65-66.
105. Baillie, The Interpretation of Religion, p. 232.
106. Ibid., p. 231.
107. See Walter Kaufmann, Critique of Religion and Philosophy, pp. 137-172; Geddes MacGregor, Introduction to Religious Philosophy, pp. 92-129; David Elton Trueblood, General Philosophy, pp. 92-111; Eric S. Waterhouse, The Philosophical Approach to Religion, pp. 59-83.
108. Baillie, The Roots of Religion in the Human Soul, p. 112.
109. Ibid., pp. 110-117. Cf. Baillie, The Interpretation of Religion, pp. 238-245, 317-320, 340-380. See also John Baillie, "The Meaning of Duty," pp. 718-730; John Baillie, "The True Ground for Theistic Belief," pp. 44-52; John Baillie, "The Logic of Religion," pp. 6-13.
110. Baillie, Our Knowledge of God, p. 143.
111. Baillie, The Sense of the Presence of God, p. 61.
112. Ibid., p. 54.
113. Ibid., pp. 52-54, 60-61.
114. Douglas Clyde Macintosh, The Problem of Religious Knowledge, p. 183.
115. Baillie, Our Knowledge of God, pp. 147-148.
116. Ibid., p. 155.
117. Ibid., pp. 157-163.
118. Baillie, The Sense of the Presence of God, pp. 17-18.
119. The best indication in the Scriptures of the personal aspect of

NOTES

God's revelation is in the Johannine usage of the Incarnated logos. The logos is not an impersonal term used to describe God's revelation but is a word that is used to convey the fact that a personal manifestation of God was revealed when the logos "became flesh" in the form of a specific man, Jesus Christ. This concept of the personal nature of God's self-disclosure is seen not only in John 1:1-16, but also in Colossians 1:12-20; Philippians 2:5-11; Hebrews 1:1-4. In the Gospel of John 5:39-40, Jesus himself said: "You search the scriptures, because you think that in them you have eternal life; and it is they that bear witness to me; yet you refuse to come to me that you may have life." Archibald Thomas Robertson notes that the rabbis, to whom Jesus refers, had made a mechanical use of the letter of Scripture as a means of salvation. But Robertson contends that "the true value of the Scriptures is in their witness to Christ (of me, peri emou)." Archibald Thomas Robertson, The Fourth Gospel; The Epistle to the Hebrews, p. 92. Is not the error that Jesus accused the rabbis of making in this passage, the same error that fundamentalism makes today in its contention that revelation is propositional? For a good discussion of the knowledge of God in the Bible see O. A. Piper, "Knowledge," The Interpreter's Dictionary of the Bible, III, pp. 42-48.

120. Although there are divergent ways of expressing it, many contemporary theologians could be listed who support the position that God's revelation is personal and not propositional. A few are indicated here. Karl Barth, Church Dogmatics, I, 1, pp. 124-135; Emil Brunner, Revelation and Reason: The Christian Doctrine of Faith and Knowledge, pp. 95-118; William Newton Clarke, An Outline of Christian Theology, pp. 9-21; Gerhard Ebeling, The Nature of Faith, pp. 84-95; Austin Farrer, The Glass of Vision, pp. 36-39; Nels F. S. Ferre, The Christian Understanding of God, pp. 154-184; Leonard Hodgson, For Faith and Freedom, I, 72-90; William Hordern, The Case for a New Reformation Theology, pp. 53-75; Edwin Lewis, The Biblical Faith and Christian Freedom, pp. 98-114; John Macquarrie, Principles of Christian Theology, pp. 75-110; Jürgen Moltmann, Theology of Hope, pp. 112-120; Wolfhart Pannenberg, Jesus, God, and Man, pp. 125-133; Eric C. Rust, Nature and Man in Biblical Thought, pp. 1-12; Frank Stagg, New Testament Theology, pp. 4-6; William Temple, Nature, Man and God, pp. 317-325; Paul Tillich, Systematic Theology, I, 122-126. For some "neo-traditionalists" who advocate revelation as being propositional in some sense see Edward John Carnell, The Case for Orthodox Theology, pp. 34, 48, 106, 140; Carl F. H. Henry, editor, Revelation and the Bible: Contemporary Evangelical Thought, pp. 7, 9, 37, 72, 90-96; James I. Packer, 'Fundamentalism' and the Word of God: Some Evangelical Principles, pp. 91-94; Bernard Ramm, Special Revelation and the Word of God, pp. 154-160.

NOTES

121. Baillie, Our Knowledge of God, p. 175.
122. Baillie, The Sense of the Presence of God, p. 17.
123. Ibid.
124. Ibid., p. 258. Cf. Baillie, The Idea of Revelation in Recent Thought, pp. 91-100; The Interpretation of Religion, pp. 159, 377-380.
125. Baillie, The Sense of the Presence of God, p. 258. Cf. Baillie, The Idea of Revelation in Recent Thought, p. 92; The Interpretation of Religion, p. 377; John Baillie, "The Predicament of Humanism," p. 115.
126. Baillie, The Idea of Revelation in Recent Thought, p. 92. Cf. Baillie, The Sense of the Presence of God, p. 258.
127. Baillie, The Interpretation of Religion, p. 377.
128. Baillie, Our Knowledge of God, p. 175.
129. Baillie, The Interpretation of Religion, pp. 377-378.
130. Baillie, A Reasoned Faith, p. 72.
131. See Carnell, op. cit., pp. 34-35, 140.
132. Baillie, The Idea of Revelation in Recent Thought, pp. 91-95. Cf. Baillie, "The Given Word: The Message of the Unvarying Gospel," p. 460.
133. Baillie, The Idea of Revelation in Recent Thought, p. 93.
134. Ibid., p. 100.
135. Ibid., p. 102.
136. H. D. Lewis, Our Experience of God, p. 53.
137. Ibid., pp. 56-58.
138. Ibid., p. 58.
139. Ibid., p. 61.
140. Ibid., pp. 89-95, 160-164.
141. Baillie, The Idea of Revelation in Recent Thought, pp. 105-107. Cf. Baillie, Our Knowledge of God, p. 185.
142. Baillie, The Idea of Revelation in Recent Thought, pp. 107-108.
143. Baillie, Our Knowledge of God, p. 50.
144. Ibid., p. 62.
145. Ibid., pp. 63-65.
146. Ibid., pp. 65-66.
147. Ibid., pp. 67-69.
148. Ibid., p. 68.
149. Ibid., p. 75.
150. Ibid., p. 73.
151. Baillie, A Reasoned Faith, pp. 42-43. For a discussion of unconscious faith see D. M. Baillie, Faith in God and Its Christian Consummation, pp. 182-188; Leonard Hodgson, The Grace of God in Faith and Philosophy, pp. 149-153.
152. John Baillie, "The Subliminal Consciousness as an Aid to the

NOTES

Interpretation of Religious Experience," p. 355.
153. Baillie, The Sense of the Presence of God, p. 90.
154. Ibid.
155. Ibid., pp. 76-79.
156. Baillie, Our Knowledge of God, pp. 83-85.
157. Ibid., pp. 92-94.
158. Ibid., p. 96.
159. Ibid., pp. 99-101.
160. Baillie, The Place of Jesus Christ in Modern Christianity, pp. 206-208.
161. Baillie, The Sense of the Presence of God, p. 193.
162. Ibid., p. 195. This passage is quoted from D. M. Baillie, God Was in Christ: An Essay on Incarnation and Atonement, pp. 190-191.
163. Baillie, The Sense of the Presence of God, p. 202.
164. Cf. John 1:1-14; John 8:58; Philippians 2:6-8; Revelation 5:6, 13:8. For a discussion concerning the correlation of revelation and salvation see Karl Barth, Church Dogmatics, II, 1, pp. 107-141; Brunner, op. cit., pp. 77-80; Edgar Primrose Dickie, God is Light: Studies in Revelation and Personal Conviction, pp. 222-236; Robinson, op. cit.; Tillich, op. cit., pp. 144-147; William J. Wolf, Man's Knowledge of God, pp. 101-113.
165. Dickie, op. cit., p. 230.
166. John Baillie, Baptism and Conversion, p. 106.
167. Ibid., pp. 106-107.
168. Ibid., p. 105. Cf. John Baillie, What is Christian Civilization?, pp. 41-47, 71-86.
169. Baillie, Our Knowledge of God, pp. 86-91.
170. Baillie, Baptism and Conversion, p. 105.
171. H. Wheeler Robinson, The Life and Faith of the Baptists, p. 73, (Italics are his).
172. George R. Beasley-Murray, Baptism in the New Testament, p. 304, (Italics are his).
173. E. Y. Mullins, The Axioms of Religion, pp. 56-57.
174. William L. Lumpkin, Baptist Confessions of Faith, p. 211.
175. Cf. the discussion by Dale Moody, Baptism: Foundation for Christian Unity, pp. 258ff.; Findley Edge, A Quest for Vitality in Religion, pp. 189ff.; Craig Ratliff, "Discipleship, Church Membership, and the Place of Children Among Southern Baptists," (unpublished doctoral thesis, Southern Baptist Seminary, 1963); and Warren Carr, Baptism: Conscience and Clue for the Church, pp. 177ff.
176. Most Baptist theologians, along with others, have employed the term "sanctification" to describe the growth of one who has made the initial

NOTES

commitment to God. E. Y. Mullins has observed that sanctification is gradual. "It is not attained in its completeness by a single act of consecration. Sanctification is a life process." Edgar Young Mullins, The Christian Religion in Its Doctrinal Expression, p. 422. Probably no Baptist has put greater emphasis on the continued necessity of growth in the Christian life after conversion than Walter Rauschenbusch. "'Sanctification,' according to almost any definition, is the continuation of that process of spiritual education and transformation by which a human personality becomes a willing organ of the spirit of Christ." Walter Rauschenbusch, A Theology for the Social Gospel, p. 102. Rauschenbusch stressed the necessity of personal experimental decision. See Walter Rauschenbusch, The Social Principles of Jesus, pp. 5, 81-89, 158-159; A Theology for the Social Gospel, pp. 95-100; Christianizing the Social Order, pp. 103-104, 460-462. Cf. Stagg, op. cit., pp. 80-121, 145-148; Robinson, Redemption and Revelation, pp. 290-297; Clarke declares that "in the process of sanctification the Holy Spirit who initiated the divine life is the ever-present agent. The Holy Spirit nourishes and strengthens the holy love that he has awakened." Clarke, op. cit., p. 409.

177. Baillie, Baptism and Conversion, p. 111.
178. Ibid., p. 112.
179. Robinson, The Life and Faith of the Baptists, p. 147.
180. Karl Barth, Church Dogmatics, Vol. IV, Part 4-Fragment, p. 164. Cf. pp. 164-195.
181. Karl Barth, The Teaching of the Church Regarding Baptism, pp. 34-54.
182. Barth, op. cit., Preface.
183. For works by Baptists who have endeavored to open the way for responsible theological dialogue with other theologians on the issue of baptism see "Baptist and Baptism" Review and Expositor, (Vol. LXV, No. 1, Winter, 1968); (This entire issue is devoted to a study of Baptism). George R. Beasley-Murray, Baptism in the New Testament; Warren Carr, Baptism: Conscience and Clue for The Church; W. F. Flemington, "Baptism," The Interpreter's Dictionary of the Bible, pp. 348-353 and The New Testament Doctrine of Baptism; Alec Gilmore, editor, Christian Baptism; Dale Moody, Baptism: Foundation for Christian Unity; H. H. Rowley, "The Origin and Meaning of Baptism," The Baptist Quarterly (London: The Carey Kingsgate Press, Ltd., 1942-45), and T. C. Smith, "The Doctrine of Baptism in the New Testament," in What Is The Church? edited by Duke K. McCall.

For a partial list of other scholars who have examined the doctrine of baptism and its practice see Kurt Aland, Did the Early Church Baptize Infants? D. S. Bailey, Sponsors at Baptism and Confirmation; G. W.

NOTES

Bromiley, Baptism and the Anglican Reformers and The Baptism of Infants; Oscar Cullmann, Baptism in The New Testament; Joachim Jeremias, Infant Baptism in The First Four Centuries; and Albrecht Oepke, "βάπτω, βαπτίζω, βαπτισμός, βάπτισμα," pp. 529-545, Theological Dictionary of the New Testament, edited by Gerhard Kittel.

CHAPTER FOUR

1. John Baillie, The Idea of Revelation in Recent Thought, p. 110.
2. Ibid., pp. 62-66, 117-125. Cf. John Baillie, The Belief in Progress, pp. 66-74; John Baillie, Invitation to Pilgrimage, pp. 79-80.
3. Baillie, The Idea of Revelation in Recent Thought, p. 110.
4. John Baillie, The Interpretation of Religion, p. 464.
5. John Baillie, The Place of Jesus Christ in Modern Christianity, p. 114.
6. Baillie, The Idea of Revelation in Recent Thought, pp. 78-82, 125. Cf. John Baillie, Our Knowledge of God, pp. 180-189; John Baillie, "The Given Word: The Message of the Unvarying Gospel," pp. 459-460. See John 5:39; John 20:30-31.
7. Although Bernard Ramm believes that the expression "propositional revelation" is a prejudiced one, he frankly acknowledges that he accepts in principle what its critics intend by the phrase. For his discussion of this phrase see Bernard Ramm, Special Revelation and the Word of God, pp. 154-160. Cf. Carl F. H. Henry, editor, Revelation and the Bible: Contemporary Evangelical Thought, pp. 90-104; Edward John Carnell, The Case for Orthodox Theology, pp. 34-35, 140-141; William Hordern, The Case for a New Reformation Theology, pp. 53-75; William Temple, Nature, Man and God, pp. 301-327.
8. Baillie, "The Given Word: The Message of the Unvarying Gospel," p. 459.
9. Baillie, The Idea of Revelation in Recent Thought, p. 66.
10. Baillie, The Place of Jesus Christ in Modern Christianity, p. 113.
11. Baillie, The Interpretation of Religion, p. 464, f.n.
12. Baillie, The Idea of Revelation in Recent Thought, pp. 110-111.
13. Ibid., pp. 111-112.
14. Ibid., pp. 115-116.
15. Ibid.
16. Ibid., pp. 124-125. Cf. Baillie, Our Knowledge of God, p. 235. Leonard Hodgson has noted that "the theory of plenary inspiration has never been literally applied in a thoroughgoing fashion by responsible theologians. That has been left to the world of comic fiction." Leonard Hodgson, For Faith and Freedom, I, 72.

NOTES

17. Dewey M. Beegle, The Inspiration of Scripture, p. 79.
18. Baillie, The Idea of Revelation in Recent Thought, p. 125.
19. John Baillie, The Sense of the Presence of God, p. 92.
20. Baillie, The Idea of Revelation in Recent Thought, pp. 116-117.
21. Baillie, The Sense of the Presence of God, pp. 92-93.
22. Baillie, The Idea of Revelation in Recent Thought, pp. 117-119.
23. C. H. Dodd, The Authority of the Bible, p. 297.
24. Ibid., p. 300. Hodgson has observed that those who seek to rest their position on the fact that "the Bible says" are trying to ascribe to the Bible an ultimate authority which can only rightly be found in God himself. Leonard Hodgson, For Faith and Freedom, II, 12-21. In a discussion of the Scriptures as the source of authority, Ramm notes that the Protestant position is not one of a "paper pope." He sets forth his observation in the following manner: "Christianity has existed without Scripture in the past, and it exists today without Scripture among primitives who have heard the gospel but cannot read it in a Bible.... The total acts of God in making himself known are all revelatory, and the revelatory actions of God extend beyond Scripture. Revelation may exist without Scripture (e.g., with Abraham), but Scripture cannot exist without previous revelation." "The Witness of Scripture itself," he declares, "is that Jesus Christ is the living authority of his Church.... Calvin did not substitute an infallible Bible for an infallible pope as repeated ad nauseam. Calvin replaced the religious certitude supposedly given by the Catholic Church with a religious certitude given directly by God--the inner witness of the Holy Spirit." Bernard Ramm, "Baptists and Sources of Authority," Foundations, (I:6-15, July 1958). Cf. Robert Clyde Johnson, Authority in Protestant Theology; P. T. Forsyth, The Principle of Authority in Relation to Certainty, Sanctity, and Society: An Essay in the Philosophy of Experimental Religion.
25. Baillie, Our Knowledge of God, Preface.
26. Ibid., pp. 183-184; Cf. Baillie, The Idea of Revelation in Recent Thought, pp. 124-125.
27. Baillie, The Idea of Revelation in Recent Thought, pp. 119-125. Cf. Baillie, The Sense of the Presence of God, pp. 219-220. For a further discussion of this aspect of inspiration see Beegle, op. cit.; Dodd, op. cit.; Hodgson, For Faith and Freedom, II, 3-25.
28. Baillie, The Idea of Revelation in Recent Thought, p. 81.
29. Ibid., See J. D. A. Macnicol, "Word and Deed in the New Testament," Scottish Journal of Theology, (September 1952), pp. 247-250. Cf. Genesis 1:3; Isaiah 55:11.
30. Baillie, The Idea of Revelation in Recent Thought, pp. 80-82. Cf. Baillie, "The Given Word: The Message of the Unvarying Gospel,"

NOTES

pp. 452-466.
31. Baillie, The Idea of Revelation in Recent Thought, pp. 27-32, 123-125. Cf. Baillie, The Sense of the Presence of God, pp. 259-261.
32. Baillie, The Sense of the Presence of God, p. 10.
33. Ibid., pp. 10-11.
34. Paul Tillich, The Protestant Era, p. 14. Cf. Baillie, The Sense of the Presence of God, p. 11.
35. Cf. ante, pp. 10-16.
36. Baillie, The Sense of the Presence of God, p. 18.
37. Ibid., pp. 161-162. Cf. Baillie, The Idea of Revelation in Recent Thought, pp. 26-27.
38. Baillie, The Idea of Revelation in Recent Thought, pp. 25-26.
39. Ibid., pp. 26-27.
40. Baillie, The Place of Jesus Christ in Modern Christianity, p. 27.
41. Baillie, The Sense of the Presence of God, p. 113.
42. Ibid., pp. 115-116.
43. Ibid., pp. 117-121. Cf. Baillie, Our Knowledge of God, pp. 254-258.
44. Baillie, Our Knowledge of God, p. 254.
45. Ibid., pp. 256-258. Cf. Baillie, The Sense of the Presence of God, pp. 117-121; The Interpretation of Religion, pp. 463-466.
46. John Baillie, Review of Systematic Theology, Volume I, by Paul Tillich, p. 568. Cf. Baillie, The Sense of the Presence of God, p. 116.
47. Baillie, The Idea of Revelation in Recent Thought, p. 123. H. D. Lewis has noted that the church has often committed idolatry by trying to restrict or limit its own consciousness of God within a ritual, a creed, or the Bible. See H. D. Lewis, Our Experience of God, pp. 84-103, 157-164; Cf. Hodgson, For Faith and Freedom, II, 12-25; Paul Tillich, Theology of Culture, pp. 53-67; Paul Tillich, Dynamics of Faith, pp. 41-54.
48. Baillie, The Sense of the Presence of God, p. 18.
49. Ibid., p. 161.
50. Cf. ante, p. 140.
51. Baillie, The Sense of the Presence of God, p. 150.
52. Ibid., pp. 150-151.
53. Ibid., p. 153.
54. For a discussion of the impact of the philosophy of analysis on contemporary philosophical and theological thought see Alfred Jules Ayer, Language, Truth, and Logic; Fritz Buri, How Can We Still Speak Responsibly of God? Gerhard Ebeling, Word and Faith; Frederick Ferré, Language, Logic, and God; Antony Flew and Alasdair MacIntyre, editors, New Essays in Philosophical Theology; Langdon Gilkey, Naming the

NOTES

Whirlwind: The Renewal of God-Language; John Hick, editor, The Existence of God; William Hordern, Speaking of God: The Nature and Purpose of Theological Language; C. E. M. Joad, A Critique of Logical Positivism; John Macquarrie, Principles of Christian Theology; Basil Mitchell, editor, Faith and Logic: Oxford Essays in Philosophical Theology; Ludwig Wittgenstein, Philosophical Investigations.

55. Baillie, The Sense of the Presence of God, pp. 25-27.
56. Ibid., p. 27.
57. Ibid., p. 52.
58. Ibid., pp. 52-53.
59. Ibid., pp. 52-54.
60. Ayer, op. cit., p. 71.
61. Ibid., p. 93.
62. Baillie, The Sense of the Presence of God, p. 63.
63. Ibid., pp. 63-64. Cf. Baillie, "The True Ground of Theistic Belief," pp. 51-52.
64. Baillie, The Sense of the Presence of God, p. 67.
65. Ibid., p. 68.
66. Baillie, The Interpretation of Religion, pp. 48, 34-35, 372. Cf. John Baillie, "The Present Situation in Theology," p. 20.
67. John Baillie, Natural Science and the Spiritual Life, p. 17.
68. Baillie, The Interpretation of Religion, pp. 40-48.
69. F. H. Bradley, The Principles of Logic, I, 256-261. Cf. Baillie, The Interpretation of Religion, p. 359.
70. Susanne K. Langer, Philosophy in a New Key: A Study in the Symbolism of Reason, Rite, and Art, pp. 79-102. For a discussion of the limits and weaknesses of verificational analysis see Ferré, op. cit., pp. 42-57; Joad, op. cit.; David Elton Trueblood, Philosophy of Religion, pp. 195-199.
71. Brian Gerrish, "A Conversation Resumed: Some Reflections on Recent Linguistic Philosophy," Union Seminary Quarterly Review, (March 1958), pp. 6-7.
72. Ibid., p. 7.
73. Trueblood, op. cit., pp. 196-197.
74. Paul Tillich, Systematic Theology, I, 105.
75. Baillie, The Sense of the Presence of God, pp. 71-73.
76. Baillie, The Sense of the Presence of God, p. 73. Cf. John Hick, Faith and Knowledge, p. 132.
77. Baillie, The Interpretation of Religion, p. 103.
78. John Baillie, "The Logic of Religion," p. 7.
79. Baillie, The Interpretation of Religion, p. 406.
80. Ibid.

NOTES

81. For a further discussion on the criterion of truth and falsity in religious faith see John C. Bennett, "Are There Tests of Revelation?" Theology Today, (April 1955), pp. 68-84; Langdon B. Gilkey, "A New Linguistic Madness," New Theology No. 2, Martin E. Marty and Dean G. Peerman, editors, pp. 39-49; Gerry Gill, "Talk About Religious Talk," New Theology No. 4, Martin Marty and Dean Peerman, editors; John Hick, "Theology and Verification," Theology Today, (April 1960); Hodgson, For Faith and Freedom, I, 91-93; John Macquarrie, "How is Theology Possible?" New Theology No. I, Martin E. Marty and Dean G. Peerman, editors, pp. 21-33.

CHAPTER FIVE
1. John Baillie, The Sense of the Presence of God, p. 132.
2. Ibid., pp. 132-135.
3. John Baillie, The Idea of Revelation in Recent Thought, pp. 49-50.
4. Ibid., pp. 50-52.
5. Ibid., p. 52. Cf. Baillie, The Sense of the Presence of God, pp. 135-136.
6. John Baillie, A Reasoned Faith, p. 167. "And we are witnesses to all that he did both in the country of the Jews and in Jerusalem. They put him to death by hanging him on a tree; but God raised him on the third day and made him manifest; not to all the people but to us who were chosen by God as witnesses, who ate and drank with him after he rose from the dead. And he commanded us to preach to the people, and to testify that he is the one ordained by God to be judge of the living and the dead. To him all the prophets bear witness that every one who believes in him receives forgiveness of sins through his name." Acts 10:39-43.
7. Baillie, The Idea of Revelation in Recent Thought, pp. 54-55.
8. Baillie, The Sense of the Presence of God, p. 137.
9. Ibid.
10. Ibid., p. 138.
11. Ibid., pp. 138-139.
12. John Baillie, Our Knowledge of God, pp. 179-180. Cf. Baillie, The Sense of the Presence of God, p. 139.
13. John Baillie, editor, God's Will in Our Time, pp. 16-17.
14. Baillie, The Sense of the Presence of God, p. 139.
15. Baillie, A Reasoned Faith, pp. 12-20. Cf. John Baillie, Christian Devotion, p. 80.
16. Baillie, The Sense of the Presence of God, pp. 140-141. Cf. John Baillie, Invitation to Pilgrimage, p. 146.
17. J. S. Whale, Christian Doctrine, pp. 119-120. Probably no one put greater emphasis on the corporate aspect of human life than did Walter

NOTES

Rauschenbusch. This concept is evident in all of his works, but see especially A Theology for the Social Gospel, pp. 45-56, 95-109. Cf. also Matthew 25:34-40, John 4:20-21.
18. Baillie, The Sense of the Presence of God, p. 144.
19. Ibid., pp. 144-145. Cf. John Baillie, And the Life Everlasting, pp. 159-161.
20. Baillie, The Sense of the Presence of God, p. 146.
21. Ibid., pp. 145-148.
22. Baillie, The Idea of Revelation in Recent Thought, p. 80.
23. Baillie, A Reasoned Faith, pp. 21-28.
24. Baillie, And the Life Everlasting, p. 188.
25. Ibid., p. 163.
26. Ibid., pp. 187-195.
27. Ibid., p. 196.
28. Ibid., pp. 196-226.
29. Ibid., p. 227.
30. Baillie, The Sense of the Presence of God, pp. 150-153. Cf. Baillie, The Interpretation of Religion, pp. 318-320.
31. John Baillie, "Confessions of a Transplanted Scot," pp. 54-55. Cf. Baillie, The Interpretation of Religion, pp. 318-320.
32. Baillie, The Interpretation of Religion, p. 318.
33. Baillie, The Roots of Religion in the Human Soul, p. 60.
34. Ibid., pp. 62-63. Cf. John Baillie, "The Logic of Religion," pp. 12-14; John Baillie, "The Meaning of Duty," pp. 718-720.
35. Baillie, The Roots of Religion in the Human Soul, p. 84. Cf. Baillie, The Sense of the Presence of God, pp. 138-142.
36. Baillie, The Interpretation of Religion, pp. 117, 257, 390, 461-462.
37. Baillie, The Sense of the Presence of God, pp. 88-90. Cf. Baillie, The Interpretation of Religion, pp. 246, 390-392; "The Logic of Religion," p. 11.
38. Baillie, The Roots of Religion in the Human Soul, pp. 115-116. Cf. Baillie, Our Knowledge of God, p. 162; The Interpretation of Religion, pp. 462-464.
39. See Baillie, "The True Ground of Theistic Belief," pp. 44-52; "The Logic of Religion," pp. 10-13; "The Meaning of Duty," pp. 718-730; The Interpretation of Religion, pp. 317-320.
40. Baillie, "The Meaning of Duty," p. 718.
41. Baillie, "The True Ground of Theistic Belief," pp. 51-52.
42. Ibid., p. 52.
43. Baillie, Our Knowledge of God, pp. 155-165. Cf. Baillie, The Sense of the Presence of God, pp. 140-144.

NOTES

44. H. D. Lewis, Our Experience of God, pp. 273-274.
45. Cf. ante. pp. 114-119.
46. John Baillie, "Belief As an Element in Religion," p. 80. Cf. Baillie, Our Knowledge of God, pp. 161-164; The Interpretation of Religion, pp. 312-318.
47. John Baillie, "The Predicament of Humanism," p. 115. Cf. Baillie, The Idea of Revelation in Recent Thought, pp. 100-104; The Interpretation of Religion, p. 377; Our Knowledge of God, p. 175.
48. Matthew 25:34-40.
49. I John 4:20-21.
50. Cf. Martin Buber, I and Thou.
51. See Jeremiah 22:15-16; Amos 5:21-24; Micah 6:6-8; Matthew 7:31; James 1:27, 2:14-26.
52. Baillie, The Sense of the Presence of God, pp. 130-134.
53. Ibid., pp. 146-148.
54. Baillie, The Interpretation of Religion, p. 299.
55. Baillie, A Reasoned Faith, pp. 172-173.
56. Baillie, Our Knowledge of God, pp. 157-165.
57. Baillie, The Sense of the Presence of God, p. 236.
58. Baillie, The Idea of Revelation in Recent Thought, p. 135.
59. Ibid., p. 139.
60. Ibid., pp. 139-140.
61. Ibid., pp. 141-143.
62. John Baillie, The Human Situation, pp. 23-24.
63. Baillie, The Idea of Revelation in Recent Thought, pp. 142-145. Cf. Baillie, Christian Devotion, pp. 31-38.
64. Baillie, Christian Devotion, p. 59.
65. Baillie, The Interpretation of Religion, pp. 159, 377-380. Cf. Baillie, The Sense of the Presence of God, p. 258; Invitation to Pilgrimage, pp. 28-30; The Idea of Revelation in Recent Thought, pp. 91-100.
66. Baillie, The Idea of Revelation in Recent Thought, pp. 145-148.
67. Baillie, The Interpretation of Religion, p. 350.
68. Baillie, Our Knowledge of God, pp. 157-161.

SELECTED BIBLIOGRAPHY

A. WRITINGS OF JOHN BAILLIE

1. Books

Baillie, John, And the Life Everlasting. New York: Charles Scribner's Sons, 1933. 350 pp.

———, Baptism and Conversion. New York: Charles Scribner's Sons, 1963. 121 pp.

———, The Belief in Progress. New York: Charles Scribner's Sons, 1951. 240 pp.

———, Christian Devotion. New York: Charles Scribner's Sons, 1962. 119 pp.

———, A Diary of Private Prayer. New York: Charles Scribner's Sons, 1949. 135 pp.

———, editor, A Diary of Readings. New York: Charles Scribner's Sons, 1955. 385 pp.

———, editor, God's Will in Our Time. London: S. C. M. Press, 1946. 189 pp.

———, The Human Situation. London: Longmans, Green and Company, 1950. 28 pp.

———, The Idea of Revelation in Recent Thought. New York: Columbia University Press, 1956. 151 pp.

———, The Interpretation of Religion: An Introductory Study of Theological Principles. Edinburgh: T. and T. Clark, 1929. 477 pp.

———, Invitation to Pilgrimage. Harmondsworth, Middlesex: Penguin Books, Limited, 1960. 158 pp.

———, John T. McNeill, and Henry P. Van Dusen, editors, The Library of Christian Classics. 26 vols.; Philadelphia: The Westminster Press, 1950-57.

———, The Mind of the Modern University. London: S. C. M. Press, 1946. 36 pp.

———, Natural Science and the Spiritual Life. New York: Charles Scribner's Sons, 1952. 43 pp.

———, Our Knowledge of God. New York: Charles Scribner's Sons, 1959. 263 pp.

———, The Place of Jesus Christ in Modern Christianity. New York: Charles Scribner's Sons, 1929. 219 pp.

———, The Prospects of Spiritual Renewal. London: Oxford University Press, 1943. 63 pp.

———, A Reasoned Faith. New York: Charles Scribner's Sons, 1963. 180 pp.

Baillie, John and Hugh Martin, editors, Revelation. New York: The Macmillan Company, 1937. 312 pp.

———, The Roots of Religion in the Human Soul. Reprint; London: James Clarke and Company, Limited, 1937. 123 pp.

———, The Sense of the Presence of God. New York: Charles Scribner's Sons, 1962. 269 pp.

———, Spiritual Religion. London: George Allen and Unwin, (n.d.). 26 pp.

———, What is Christian Civilization? Second edition; London: Christophers, 1947. 88 pp.

2. Essays, Articles and Sermons in Symposiums

Baillie, John, "Confessions of a Transplanted Scot," Contemporary American Theology: Theological Autobiographies, edited by Vergilius Ferm. Second series; New York: Round Table Press, 1933. 376 pp.

———, "Divine Overruling," Best Sermons: 1947-1948 Edition, edited by G. Paul Butler. New York: Harper and Brothers Publishers, 1947. 318 pp.

———, "Donald: A Brother's Impression," in The Theology of the Sacraments and Other Papers, by D. M. Baillie. New York: Charles Scribner's Sons, 1957. 158 pp.

———, "The Fellowship of the Redemptive Quest," The Healing of the Nation, edited by J. W. Stevenson. Edinburgh: T. and T. Clark, 1930. 239 pp.

———, "Hope and Disenchantment," Best Sermons: 1949-1950 Edition, edited by G. Paul Butler. New York: Harper and Brothers Publishers, 1949. 325 pp.

———, "Was He Really the Founder," Contemporary Thinking About Jesus, edited by Thomas S. Kepler. New York: Abingdon Press, 1949. 289 pp.

3. Periodical Articles

Baillie, John, "Belief As an Element in Religion," The Expositer, 9:75-92, January 1915.

———, "Beware the Whitewash," The Christian Century, 68:1248-1249, October 31, 1951.

———, "Faith and the Scientific Impulse," Theology Today, 9:304-305, October 1952.

———, "The Fundamental Task of the Theological Seminary," The Reformed Church Review, 1:259-275, July 1922.

———, "The Given Word: The Message of the Unvarying Gospel,"

Baillie, John, "Happiness Once More," The Hibbert Journal, 26:69-83, October 1927.

———, "The Idea of Orthodoxy," The Hibbert Journal, 24:232-249, January 1926.

———, "The Logic of Religion," Alumni Bulletin of Union Theological Seminary, 3:6-16, October 1930.

———, "Looking Before and After," The Christian Century, 75:400-402, April 2, 1958.

———, "The Meaning of Duty: A Plea for a Reconsideration of the Kantian Ethic," The Hibbert Journal, 24:718-730, July 1926.

———, "The Mind of Christ on the Treatment of Crime," The Expository Times, 41:261-265, March 1930.

———, "The Predicament of Humanism," The Canadian Journal of Religious Thought, 11:109-118, March 1931.

———, "The Present Situation in Theology," Auburn Seminary Record, 3:209-229, November 1920.

———, "The Psychological Point of View," The Philosophical Review, 39:258-274, May 1930.

———, Review of Systematic Theology, Volume I, by Paul Tillich, Theology Today, 8:566-568, January 1952.

———, "Some Comments on Professor Hick's Article on 'The Christology of D. M. Baillie,'" Scottish Journal of Theology, 11:265-270, September 1958.

———, "Some Reflections on the Changing Theological Scene," Union Seminary Quarterly Review, 12:3-9, January 1957.

———, "The Subliminal Consciousness as an Aid to the Interpretation of Religious Experience," The Expository Times, 24:353-358, October 1912-September 1913.

———, "Theology Course as a Preparation for the Missionary," The International Review of Missions, 28:535-548, October 1939.

———, "The Theology of the War," The Christian Century, 60:354-356, March 24, 1943.

———, "The True Ground of Theistic Belief," The Hibbert Journal, 21:44-52, October 1922.

———, "Why I Believe in God," Union Seminary Quarterly Review, 3:3-6, March 1948.

———, "World Mission of the Church: The Contemporary Scene," The International Review of Missions, 41:161-169, April 1952.

———, "The Young Minister and the Modern Situation," The Methodist Review, 114:151-156, March 1931.

B. SELECTED SOURCES

1. Books

Ayer , Alfred Jules, Language, Truth, and Logic, New Dover edition; New York: Dover Publications, Incorporated, /n.d./. 160 pp.
Baillie , D. M., Faith in God and Its Christian Consummation. Edinburgh: T. and T. Clark, 1927. 314 pp.
_____ , God Was in Christ: An Essay on Incarnation and Atonement. New York: Charles Scribner's Sons, 1948. 230 pp.
Barr , James, The Semantics of Biblical Language. London: Oxford University Press, 1961. 313 pp.
Barth , Karl, The Doctrine of the Word of God. Vol. I, Part 1 of Church Dogmatics, translated by G. T. Thomson. Edinburgh: T. and T. Clark, 1956. 575 pp.
_____ , The Doctrine of the Word of God. Vol. I, Part 2 of Church Dogmatics, translated by G. T. Thomson. Edinburgh: T. and T. Clark, 1956. 905 pp.
_____ , The Doctrine of God. Vol. II, Part 1 of Church Dogmatics, translated by T. H. Parker, et. al. Edinburgh: T. and T. Clark, 1957. 699 pp.
_____ , The Doctrine of God. Vol. II, Part 2 of Church Dogmatics, translated by G. W. Bromiley, et. al. Edinburgh: T. and T. Clark, 1957. 806 pp.
_____ , The Doctrine of Creation. Vol. III, Part 1 of Church Dogmatics, translated by J. W. Edwards, et. al. Edinburgh: T. and T. Clark, 1958. 428 pp.
_____ , The Doctrine of Creation. Vol. III, Part 2 of Church Dogmatics, translated by Harold Knight, et. al. Edinburgh: T. and T. Clark, 1960. 661 pp.
_____ , The Doctrine of Reconciliation. Vol. IV, Part 1 of Church Dogmatics, translated by G. W. Bromiley. Edinburgh: T. and T. Clark, 1956. 802 pp.
_____ , The Doctrine of Reconciliation. Vol. IV, Part 2 of Church Dogmatics, translated by G. W. Bromiley. Edinburgh: T. and T. Clark, 1958. 867 pp.
_____ , The Epistle to the Romans, translated by Edwin C. Hoskyns. Sixth edition; London: Oxford University Press, 1957. 547 pp.
_____ , The Humanity of God, translated by Thomas Weiser and John Newton Thomas. Richmond: John Knox Press, 1960. 96 pp.
_____ , The Teaching of the Church Regarding Baptism, translated by Ernest A. Payne. London: S. C. M. Press, 1948. 64 pp.
_____ , The Word of God and the Word of Man, translated by Douglas

Beasley - Murray, George R., *Baptism in the New Testament*. London: Macmillan & Co., Ltd., 1962. 393 pp.

Beegle, Dewey M., *The Inspiration of Scripture*. Philadelphia: The Westminster Press, 1963. 223 pp.

Bendall, Kent, and Frederick Ferré, *Exploring the Logic of Faith: A Dialogue on the Relation of Modern Philosophy to Christian Faith*. New York: Association Press, 1962. 219 pp.

Bradley, F. H., *The Principles of Logic*. Second edition, revised and reprinted; London: Oxford University Press, 1950. 2 vols. 739 pp.

Brunner, Emil, *The Divine-Human Encounter*, translated by Amandus W. Loos. Philadelphia: The Westminster Press, 1943. 207 pp.

_____, *Revelation and Reason: The Christian Doctrine of Faith and Knowledge*, translated by Olive Wyon. Philadelphia: The Westminster Press, 1946. 440 pp.

Buber, Martin, *I and Thou*, translated by Ronald Gregor Smith. New York: Charles Scribner's Sons, 1957. 120 pp.

Carnell, Edward John, *The Case for Orthodox Theology*. Philadelphia: The Westminster Press, 1959. 162 pp.

Conner, Walter Thomas, *Revelation and God: An Introduction to Christian Doctrine*. Nashville, Tennessee: Broadman Press, 1936. 354 pp.

DeWolf, L. Harold, *The Case for Theology in Liberal Perspective*. Philadelphia: The Westminster Press, 1959. 206 pp.

_____, *The Religious Revolt Against Reason*. New York: Harper and Brothers Publishers, 1949. 217 pp.

_____, *A Theology of the Living Church*. Revised edition; New York: Harper and Brothers Publishers, 1960. 383 pp.

Dickie, Edgar Primrose, *God Is Light: Studies in Revelation and Personal Conviction*. New York: Charles Scribner's Sons, 1954. 261 pp.

_____, *Revelation and Response*. New York: Charles Scribner's Sons, 1938. 278 pp.

Dodd, C. H., *The Authority of the Bible*. Revised and reprinted; London: Nisbet and Company, Limited, 1955. 310 pp.

Driver, S. R., *The Book of Genesis*, in *Westminster Commentaries*, edited by Walter Lock. Second edition; London: Methuen and Company, 1904. 420 pp.

Ferré, Frederick, *Language, Logic, and God*. New York: Harper and Brothers Publishers, 1961. 184 pp.

Ferré, Nels F. S., *The Christian Understanding of God*. New York: Harper and Brothers Publishers, 1951. 277 pp.

Ferré, Nels F. S., Faith and Reason. New York: Harper and Brothers Publishers, 1946. 251 pp.

Flew, Antony, and Alasdair Macintyre, editors, New Essays in Philosophical Theology. London: S. C. M. Press, Limited, 1961. 274 pp.

Forsyth, P. T., The Principle of Authority in Relation to Certainty, Sanctity, and Society: An Essay in the Philosophy of Experimental Religion. Second edition; London: Independent Press, Limited, 1952. 430 pp.

Foster, Michael B., Mystery and Philosophy. London: S. C. M. Press, Limited, 1957. 96 pp.

Gilkey, Langdon, Naming the Whirlwind: The Renewal of God-Language. Indianapolis: Bobbs-Merrill Co., 1969. 483 pp.

Gilson, Etienne, Reason and Revelation in the Middle Ages. New York: Charles Scribner's Sons, 1938. 114 pp.

Harkness, Georgia, Foundations of Christian Knowledge. New York: Abingdon Press, 1955. 160 pp.

Hazelton, Roger, On Proving God: A Handbook in Christian Conversation. New York: Harper and Brothers Publishers, 1952. 186 pp.

Henry, Carl F. H., editor, Revelation and the Bible: Contemporary Evangelical Thought. London: The Tyndale Press, 1959. 413 pp.

Hick, John, Faith and Knowledge: A Modern Introduction to the Problem of Religious Knowledge. Ithaca, New York: Cornell University Press, 1957. 221 pp.

Hodgson, Leonard, For Faith and Freedom, I. Oxford: Basil Blackwell, 1956. 241 pp.

_____, For Faith and Freedom, II. Oxford: Basil Blackwell, 1957. 237 pp.

_____, The Grace of God in Faith and Philosophy. London: Longmans, Green and Company, 1936. 182 pp.

Hordern, William, The Case for A New Reformation Theology. Philadelphia: The Westminster Press, 1959. 176 pp.

Horton, Walter Marshall, Christian Theology: An Ecumenical Approach. Revised and enlarged edition; New York: Harper and Brothers Publishers, 1958. 320 pp.

Joad, C. E. M., A Critique of Logical Positivism. Chicago: University of Chicago Press, 1950. 154 pp.

Johnson, Robert Clyde, Authority in Protestant Theology. Philadelphia: The Westminster Press, 1959. 224 pp.

Jones, Rufus M., The New Quest. New York: The Macmillan Company, 1928. 202 pp.

Knudson, Albert C., The Religious Teaching of the Old Testament. New York: Abingdon Press, 1918. 416 pp.

Koehler, Ludwig, <u>Old Testament Theology,</u> translated by A. S. Todd. London: Lutterworth Press, 1957. 259 pp.

Langer, Susanne K., <u>Philosophy in a New Key: A Study in the Symbolism of Reason, Rite, and Art.</u> Cambridge, Massachusetts: Harvard University Press, 1942. 313 pp.

Lewis, Edwin, <u>A Philosophy of the Christian Revelation.</u> New York: Harper and Brothers Publishers, 1940. 356 pp.

Lewis, H. D., <u>Our Experience of God.</u> London: George Allen and Unwin, Limited, 1959. 301 pp.

Lumpkin, W. L., <u>Baptist Confessions of Faith,</u> Philadelphia: The Judson Press, 1959. 430 pp.

Macquarrie, John, <u>Twentieth Century Religious Thought: The Frontiers of Philosophy and Theology, 1900-1960.</u> New York: Harper and Row Publishers, 1963. 415 pp.

Mitchell, Basil, editor, <u>Faith and Logic: Oxford Essays in Philosophical Theology.</u> London: George Allen and Unwin, Limited, 1957. 222 pp.

Mozley, John Kenneth, <u>Some Tendencies in British Theology: From the Publications of Lux Mundi to the Present Day.</u> London: S. P. C. K., 1952. 166 pp.

Mullins, E. Y., <u>The Axioms of Religion.</u> Philadelphia: The Judson Press, 1908. 98 pp.

_____, <u>The Christian Religion in Its Doctrinal Expression.</u> Philadelphia: The Judson Press, 1954. 514 pp.

Niebuhr, H. Richard, <u>The Meaning of Revelation.</u> New York: The Macmillan Company, 1941. 196 pp.

Orr, James, <u>Revelation and Inspiration.</u> Grand Rapids: Wm. B. Eerdmans Publishing Company, 1952. 224 pp.

Pannenberg, Wolfhart, <u>Jesus-God and Man,</u> translated by Lewis L. Wilkins and Duane A. Priebe. Philadelphia: Westminster Press, 1968. 415 pp.

Packer, James I., <u>'Fundamentalism' and the Word of God: Some Evangelical Principles.</u> Reprint; Grand Rapids: Wm. B. Eerdmans Publishing Company, 1962. 191 pp.

Ramm, Bernard, <u>Special Revelation and the Word of God.</u> Grand Rapids: Wm. B. Eerdmans Publishing Company, 1961. 220 pp.

Rauschenbusch, Walter, <u>A Theology for the Social Gospel.</u> New York: The Macmillan Company, 1917. 279 pp.

Robinson, H. Wheeler, <u>The Life and Faith of the Baptists.</u> Revised edition; London: The Kingsgate Press, 1946. 158 pp.

_____, <u>Redemption and Revelation.</u> London: Nisbet and Company, Limited, 1947. 320 pp.

_____, <u>The Religious Ideas of the Old Testament.</u> Reprint of Second edition, revised by L. H. Brokington; London: Gerald

Rowley,   Duckworth and Company, Limited, 1959. 246 pp.
Rowley, H. H., <u>The Faith of Israel: Aspects of Old Testament Thought.</u> Philadelphia: The Westminster Press, 1956. 220 pp.

Rust   , Eric C., <u>Nature and Man in Biblical Thought.</u> London: Lutterworth Press, 1953. 318 pp.

Stagg   , Frank, <u>New Testament Theology.</u> Nashville, Tennessee: Broadman Press, 1962. 361 pp.

Temple, William, <u>Christ's Revelation of God.</u> London: S. C. M. Press, Limited, 1952. 63 pp.

——— , <u>Nature, Man and God.</u> London: Macmillan and Company, Limited, 1956. 530 pp.

Tillich , Paul, <u>Dynamics of Faith.</u> Harper Torchbook edition; New York: Harper and Brothers Publishers, 1958. 134 pp.

——— , <u>The Protestant Era,</u> translated by James Luther Adams. Abridged edition, Phoenix Books; Chicago: The University of Chicago Press, 1960. 242 pp.

——— , <u>Systematic Theology.</u> I. Chicago: The University of Chicago Press, 1951. 300 pp.

Trueblood, David Elton, <u>General Philosophy.</u> New York: Harper and Row Publishers, 1963. 370 pp.

——— , <u>The Knowledge of God.</u> New York: Harper and Brothers Publishers, 1939. 207 pp.

——— , <u>Philosophy of Religion.</u> New York: Harper and Brothers Publishers, 1957. 324 pp.

Waterhouse, Eric S., <u>The Philosophical Approach to Religion.</u> Revised edition; London: The Epworth Press, 1960. 194 pp.

Whale , J. S., <u>Christian Doctrine.</u> Fontana Books; London: Cambridge University Press, 1958. 190 pp.

Whitehead, A. N., <u>Adventures of Ideas.</u> Reprint; Cambridge, Massachusetts: University Press, 1947. 392 pp.

Wittgenstein, Ludwig, <u>Philosophical Investigations,</u> translated by G. E. M. Anscombe. Oxford: Basil Blackwell, 1953. 232 pp.

Wolf   , William J., <u>Man's Knowledge of God.</u> Garden City, New York: Doubleday and Company, Incorporated, 1955. 189 pp.

2. Books: Parts of Series

Rad   , Gerhard von, <u>Old Testament Theology</u> Vol. I of <u>The Theology of Israel's Historical Tradition,</u> translated by D. M. G. Stalker, New York: Harper and Brothers Publishers, 1962. 483 pp.

Robertson, Archibald Thomas, <u>The Fourth Gospel; The Epistle to the Hebrews.</u> Vol. V of <u>Word Pictures in the New Testament.</u> 6 vols.; Nashville, Tennessee: Broadman Press, 1932.

3. Periodical Articles

Bennett, John C., "Are There Tests of Revelation?" Theology Today, 12:68-84, April 1955.

Ferré, Frederick, "Is Language About God Fraudulent?" Scottish Journal of Theology, 12:337-360, December 1959.

Fey, Harold E., "Baillie Dies in Edinburgh," The Christian Century, 77:1172, October 12, 1960.

Forrester, Isobel M., "Invitation to Pilgrimage: In Memoriam--John Baillie," The International Review of Missions, 50:191-194, April 1961.

Gerrish, Brian, "A Conversation Resumed: Some Reflections on Recent Linguistic Philosophy," Union Seminary Quarterly Review, 13:3-11, March 1958.

Loos, Amandus W., "Theology in Scotland," The Christian Review, 9:101-109, April 1940.

MacKay, John A., "John Baillie, A Lyrical Tribute and Appraisal," Scottish Journal of Theology, 9:225-235, September 1956.

Mueller, David L., "The Theology of Karl Barth and the Nineteenth Century," Religion in Life, 34:81-94, Winter 1964-65.

Ramm, Bernard, "Baptists and Sources of Authority," Foundations, 1:6-15, July 1958.

Torrance, T. F., "A Living Sacrifice: In Memoriam, John Baillie, 1886-1960," Religion in Life, 30:329-333, Summer 1961.

4. Biographical, Dictionary and Encyclopedia Articles

"John Baillie," The International Who's Who 1960, 50-51.
"John Baillie," Religious Leaders of America 1941-42, II, 46.
"John Baillie," Twentieth Century Encyclopedia of Religious Knowledge: An Extension of the New Schaff-Herzog Encyclopedia of Religious Knowledge, I, 105.
"John Baillie," Who's Who 1960. 128-129.
"John Baillie," Who's Who in America 1934-1935, XVIII, 224.
Moule, C. F. D., "Revelation," The Interpreter's Dictionary of the Bible, IV, 54-58.
Piper, O. A., "Knowledge," The Interpreter's Dictionary of the Bible, III, 42-48.

5. Unpublished Materials

Braman, Clifford L., "The Philosophical Theology of John Baillie," Unpublished doctor's dissertation, New York University, New York, 1954. 269 pp.

Jenkins, Charles O., "John Baillie--Before and After Barth." Unpublished master's thesis, Southeastern Baptist Theological Seminary, Wake Forest, North Carolina, 1955. 63 pp.

INDEX OF NAMES

Aland, Kurt, 115
Aquinas, Thomas, 23, 24, 30-31, 69
Aristotle, 23, 30-31, 69, 74
Ayer, Alfred Jules, 4, 72, 73, 118

Bailey, D. S., 115
Baillie, D. M., 55, 113
Barth, Karl, i, 14-15, 16-21, 46, 59-60, 105-106, 112
Beasley-Murray, George R., 57-58, 115
Beegle, Dewey M., 64
Berdyaev, Nicolas, 22
Berkeley, George, 1, 9
Bonaventure, 69
Bradley, F. H., 74
Braithwaite, R. B., 71
Braman, Clifford, 24-25
Bromiley, G. W., 116
Brunner, Emil, 14, 20f., 46
Buber, Martin, 41
Buri, Fritz, 118
Burrows, Millar, 107

Calvin, John, 24, 117
Carnap, Rudolf, 72
Carnell, John, 112
Carr, Warren, 114, 115
Cicero, 15
Clark, William Newton, 112, 115
Cullmann, Oscar, 116

Descartes, 1
DeWolf, L. Harold, 104
Dickie, Edgar Primrose, 56
Dodd, C. H., 35, 65
Driver, S. R., 21-22

Eakin, Jr., Frank E., 107
Ebeling, Gerhard, ii, 112, 118

Edge, Findley, 114
Eichrodt, Walter, 107
Ferré, Frederick, 118, 119
Ferré, Nels, F. S., 28
Flemington, W. F., 115
Flew, Antony, 118
Forsyth, P. T., 117

Gerrish, Brian, 74-75
Gilkey, Langdon, 118-119
Gilmore, Alec, 115
Gilson, Etienne, 31

Harkness, Georgia, 13, 103
Hebert, A. G., 46
Hegel, G. W. F., 1
Henry, Carl, F. H., 112
Herrmann, Wilhelm, 17, 85
Hick, John, 119
Hodgson, Leonard, 104, 108, 113, 116, 117, 118
Hordern, William, 112, 119
Hume, David, 1, 44

Jeremias, Joachim, 116
Jesus Christ, 17f., 24, 34f., 38f., 40f., 45, 48, 51, 55ff., 61, 77, 80f., 83f., 86, 95
Joad, C. E. M., 119
Johnson, Robert Clyde, 117
Johnson, Samuel, 8
Jones, Rufus M., 9

Kant, Immanuel, 1, 16, 33, 44, 46, 85-86, 89, 94
Ker, John, 53
Kierkegaard, Søren, 46
Knudson, Albert C., 107
Koehler, Ludwig, 107

Langer, Susanne, 74

Lewis, Edwin, 112
Lewis, H. D., 49-50, 87, 118
Locke, John, 1
Luther, Martin, 17, 65

Macintosh, Douglas Clyde, 45
MacIntyre, Alasdair, 118
MacKay, John A., 32
Macmurray, John, 71
Macquarrie, John, 112, 119
McCall, Duke K., 115
McLuskey, J. Fraster, 58
Martin, C. B., 104
Mitchell, Basil, 119
Moltmann, Jürgen, ii, 112
Moody, Dale, 114
Mullins, E. Y., 58, 115

Newman, J. H., 4, 73

Oepke, Albrecht, 116

Packer, James I., 112
Pannenberg, Wolfhart, i, ii, 112
Pascal, Blaise, 33, 87
Paul, 15
Piper, O. A., 112
Plato, 15, 23, 30-31, 32, 55, 69f., 85-86
Pringle-Pattison, Andrew Seth, 85

Rad, Gerhard Von, 107
Ramm, Bernard, 112, 116, 117
Rauschenbusch, Walter, 115, 120-121
Ritschl, Albrecht, 17
Robertson, Archibald Thomas, 112
Robinson, H. Wheeler, 57-58
Rowley, H. H., 107
Russell, Bertrand, 6
Rust, Eric C., 107, 112

Smith, T. C., 115
Socrates, 55, 58

Spinoza, Baruch, 86
Stagg, Frank, ii, 107, 112
Stoics, 15, 23

Taylor, A. E., 46
Temple, William, 23-24, 35, 42, 46, 112
Tennant, Frederick R., 46
Tillich, Paul, i, 24, 76, 112
Trueblood, Elton, 1-2, 75

Vider, Alex, 58

Whale, J. S., 82
Whitehead, A. N., 3
Wittgenstein, Ludwig, 72, 74, 119

Zeno, 55

INDEX OF SUBJECTS

Absolute, The, 33, 91f.
absolute obligation, 91f.
Acts 10:39-43, 120
agape, 72, 81f., 97
analogia entis, 69f.
analysis, philosophy of, 118-119
Apostles Creed, 49
argument, function of, 33, 39, 44f.
Athanasian Creed, 49
atonement, 55

baptism, 56ff., 101, 115-116
Baptists, 57ff., 114-116
belief and morality, 87f.
Bible, 61ff., 65, 80, 96, 99f., 117, 118
biblical authority, 64f.
biblical tradition, 31f.

categorical imperative, 16
certitude, 3
challenge of revelation, 90ff., 97
Christianity, 14, 34, 86, 89
Church, 40, 52, 57, 81f., 118
cogito, ergo sum, 1
commitment, 49f., 53f., 96
communion, 50-51
consciousness of value, 33, 85ff.
content of revelation, 29f., 42, 96
continuity, 26
conversion, 56ff., 94, 101
credo ut intelligam, 24
criterion of revelation, 76ff., 89, 96, 104
criterion of truth and falsity, 120
cross, 35
Cyprianic formula, 81

Deus revelatus, 37, 68
Deus velatus, 37, 68
dialectical claim, 67f.

direct awareness, 42f., 96
direct confrontation, 9, 30
discovery and disclosure, 29
discovery and revelation, 26ff., 95, 97
divine self-disclosure, 30f.

empirical knowledge, 9
encounter, 29f., 38ff., 46f., 95, 97, 104
evil, problem of, 28
existential moment, 51
extra ecclesiam nulla salus, 40

faith, 42ff., 74, 76, 82, 96, 104
frame of reference, 79f.

general knowledge of God, 13ff., 50, 54, 94, 108
Genesis 1:3, 110
gospel, the, 79f.
Greek philosophy, 32f.
ground of all knowledge, 10-11

Heilsgeschichte, 61f., 80, 96
Hic et nunc, 51-52
historical revelation, 34f., 40, 55, 85f., 95
hope, Christian, 83f.

illative sense, 73, 96
imago dei, 16, 18-22, 24-26, 27, 94, 98
immortality, 83f.
Incarnation, 17-18, 35f., 55, 83, 95, 102, 112
inference, 7
inspiration of Scripture, 62ff., 96, 100-101, 116, 117
intuition, 44-46, 96
Isaiah 55:11, 110

Jesus Christ, 17f., 24, 34f., 38f., 40f., 45, 48, 51, 55ff., 61, 77, 80f., 83f., 86, 95
John 5:39-40, 112
I John 4:8, 51; 4:20-21, 88

kairos, 80
kerygma, 36, 62, 80
kerygmatic theology, 17
kinds of knowledge, 5-8, 67
kingdom of God, 82f.
koinōnia, 52, 71, 81f., 97

language and religious knowledge, 61ff., 118-119, 120
life, 80f.
life everlasting, 89f., 97
limitations of knowledge, 4-5
linguistic analysis, 9, 65ff., 72ff., 118-119
logic of hope, 83f.
logic of religion, 33, 83f.
logical positivism, 4, 65ff., 72ff., 96, 118-119
Logos, 37, 55, 56, 66, 102, 112

man, nature of, 16f.
Matthew 25:34-40, 88-89
mediated immediacy, 39f., 51, 95, 99
moral argument, 86
moral consciousness, 26
moral obligation, 33-34
mystery, 37f., 110

natural religion, 23-26, 94
natural theology, 30, 99
nature and grace, 25-26, 54ff.
nature of religious knowledge, 13
Nicene Creed, 49
non-sensuous perception, 10, 45, 73, 93

ordo cognoscendi, 76

paradox, 5
Parousia, 38
personal knowledge, 41-42, 112
possibility of knowledge, 1-3, 8-9, 16
practical and regulative, 89f., 97
practical reason, 46
presuppositions of knowledge, 103
principle of verification, 72ff.
proofs of God, 24, 30ff., 33ff., 44ff., 65f., 72f., 90
propositional knowledge, 39f., 42, 44, 46, 48ff., 62, 64, 73, 93, 96, 98, 112, 116, 117

rational faculty, 27, 52, 71ff., 98f.
real and putative knowledge, 4, 93
reality, 5-8, 46, 67f.
reception of revelation, 38f.
reign of God, 82f.
religious awareness, 15-16, 42f., 96
religious experience, 41f., 43f., 49f., 96, 104
revealed truths, 49-50
revelation, 4, 11, 14, 22ff., 29f., 35f., 41f., 51, 63f., 76f., 94, 104, 108

salvation, 53ff., 114
sanctification, 114-115
science, 5
special knowledge, 14-15, 29ff., 54f., 94
subconscious knowledge, 16
symbolism, 68, 71, 74, 102

tests of revelation, 76f., 104
2 Timothy 1:12, 49
trust and assent, 47ff., 87, 91f., 96
truth, 6, 67, 71f., 120
truth and relevancy, 71f.

unconscious faith, 53, 101, 113
universality of religious knowledge,
    14ff., 33f., 98

verification of religious knowledge,
    71ff., 100, 119
via dolorosa, 35
Vienna Circle, 75

ways of believing, 52-53
Word of God, 17, 37, 66f.

ABOUT THE AUTHOR

William Powell Tuck, a native of Virginia, is presently pastor of the First Baptist Church in Bristol, Virginia, and Adjunct Professor of Religion and Philosophy at Virginia Intermont College. He is a graduate of the University of Richmond; Southeastern Baptist Theological Seminary, Wake Forest, North Carolina, B.D., Th.M.; and the New Orleans Baptist Theological Seminary, Th.D. He has done additional graduate study at Emory University. In 1977 he was awarded a honorary D.D. degree from the University of Richmond. He is married and the father of a daughter and a son. Previous pastorates have been in Louisiana and Virginia. He has been active in denominational and civic affairs and serves as a trustee of Virginia Intermont College. In 1974, he was awarded the Man and Boy Award from the Bristol Boys' Club. Dr. Tuck is listed in Who's Who in Religion, 1977, and the Dictionary of International Biography. He is a member of the American Academy of Religion, and the Virginia Philosophical Association. He is the author of Facing Grief and Death, which was published in 1975, a contributor and editor of The Struggle For Meaning, published in 1977, and contributor to several other works. He has had articles published in magazines, such as Theology Today, The Review and Expositor, The New Pulpit Digest, and other publications.

K

LIBRARY OF DAVIDSON COLLEGE

Books on regular loan may be checked out for **two weeks**. Books must be presented at the Circulation Desk in order to be renewed.

A fine is charged after date due.

Special books are subject to special regulations at the discretion of the library staff.

MAY -3 1989